BREAKING IDEAS

TRACKING THE ORIGIN OF IDEAS & INNOVATION

AADHITHYA

Made with ♥ on the Notion Press Platform
www.notionpress.com

I would like to dedicate this book to the visionary Dr. A.P.J. Abdul Kalam, who has been a beacon of inspiration to people across the world. He was a firm believer in the power of dreams and the relentless pursuit of knowledge paving way for innovations and ground breaking ideas in various fields of science & technology.

Dr. Kalam, who started from nothing, showed us that being very kind, never giving up, and always being curious can change a person. Before he was India's Missile Man or even the People's President, he was simply an ordinary person but then, he did many things in aerospace engineering and played a large part in India's space and missile technology. What's more, he meant very much to young people, urging them to go beyond their boundaries with technology. His life was naturally a story where hard work and passion might well end up in important achievements.

In his own words, "Dream, dream, dream. Dreams transform into thoughts and thoughts result in action." This is what this book is all about. It's a testament to nurturing ideas, tracking their origins, and turning them into innovations that can change the world.

This book's a call to Dr. Kalam's spirit that just won't quit, urging all of us to delve into the new and chase after the if's even if they're scary or unknown. His undercurrent of always pushing boundaries and believing we can do the impossible keeps reminding everyone to aim for great things. It's meant to excite everyone to always think about great things they want to do and come up with fresh ideas, showing how those dreams are inherently similar to what Dr. Kalam stood for.

My sincere gratitude goes out to Dr. Kalam, for his unwavering dedication to science and technology and for guiding innovators everywhere.

Contents

Preface

Once upon a time when I was studying my Mechanical Engineering in the college I was wondering how will I get placed in a good company from the college since the number of companies coming and recruiting were in single digit numbers and the number of students waiting to be recruited were in 3 digits, that is when I thought I would have to do something different from the crowd to stand out. That is when I stumbled upon crowdsourcing and innovation, this gave me an opportunity to solve real world problems, get recognition, get decent travel opportunities and a side income too.

This book will help people to think out ideas and innovate, throughout this book I would like to share my experiences solving innovation challenges, the best practices, the things that didn't work and how I managed to win 60+ global innovation challenges till date. You can become an Innovation consultant once you have mastered the skills of problem solving. There are always thousands of companies looking for solution to various problems, so if you can come up with solutions to help them, they will reward you, it's that simple. By the time you reach the end of this book, you should be able to think out more ideas both quantitatively and qualitatively as you will know where exactly ideas originate and ways to stimulate ideas, you might have thought earlier that great idea comes to you by chance, however later in the book you will realize that ideation is a step-by-step process and innovation is a skill which can be mastered.

I would also like to add few quick words about what I do, at the time of writing this book I work in the technology team of a proptech company. I did my bachelors in Mechanical engineering from Bangalore Institute of technology and then went on do my masters in operations management from IGNOU, during covid-19 I did my micro masters in managing technology & Innovation from RWTH University Germany. I am also the founder of an Innovation portal called Givemechallenge.com which aggregates various innovation opportunities across the world.

Acknowledgements

In the name of God, I embark on this journey of gratitude, reflecting on the profound blessings and guidance that have shaped my path. With a heart full of reverence and appreciation, I dedicate these words to those who have walked alongside me, lifted me up, and illuminated my way.

To my loving parents, I wouldn't be where I am today without your constant love and encouragement. You've been my cheerleaders, my guiding stars, and my biggest believers. Every step of this journey has been lit by your unwavering support, and for that, I am endlessly grateful.

To my amazing teachers, By teachers I mean here anyone who has taught me a lesson, pun intended, whether it is my gym trainer, swimming trainer, surfing trainer and everyone who has imparted some skill or knowledge in me. You've done so much more than teach me subjects; you've ignited a passion for learning within me. Your patience and dedication have shaped not just my mind, but also my character. I owe so much of who I am today to the lessons you've imparted.

To my mentors, Your guidance has been the compass guiding me through the ups and downs of this writing journey. Your advice, wisdom, and encouragement have been invaluable, helping me navigate challenges. I am deeply thankful for your belief in me and the impact you've had on my life and career.

And to my incredible friends, You've been my rocks, my sounding boards, and my partners in crime. Your unwavering support, laughter, and late-night brainstorming sessions have been the heartbeat of this journey. This book is dedicated to each and every one of you, with boundless gratitude and appreciation for your unwavering support, guidance, and friendship.

CHAPTER I

Where does ideas generate, essentials for successful idea generation?

Origin of ideas

Did you ever think why some people are able to think out and come up with more innovative ideas than others, you might have also observed that you get ideas through a combination of internal and external stimuli.

Thinking out ideas is a skill that can be mastered, you can download infinite number of ideas into your brain, we have to provide the infrastructure within our body and surroundings to download these ideas.

Let us compare the analogy of a smartphone phone and compare it with our body and mind, just like we have an internet through which we download ideas and information, our mind can tap into something known as Akashic records, it is a term commonly used to describe the concept of a cosmic data warehouse or repository of all knowledge, thoughts, words, emotions and intent have ever occurred in the past, present or the future.

A famous American scientist and philosopher Ervin Laszlo describes the Akashic Field as a constant memory of the universe. This zero-point Akashic Field is the record of everything that has happened and will happen in the cosmos, on Earth, and in life.

Another way to look at Akashic records would be to compare it with a memory card, if you take a picture then you need space to store it, similarly the log file of all the information in the universe including what images you have stored in your memory card need to exist perpetually in an indestructible and infinite storage repository in the universe. However, it's important to note that the idea of Akashic records is a matter of belief and interpretation rather than something that can be proven, I would encourage the readers to think more about the storage of all the information in the Universe, this will give you more clarity, you can apply your data science concepts here, data retrieval, ETL, Backup etc.

Our mind can tap into these Akashic record to download ideas, thoughts, information directly to our brain. In case of a smartphone, you would need a carrier or network to download these data packets. In case of our body the carrier is the waves that carry information from the Akasha to our subconscious which is all around us, they travel the same way the information we send through the internet travels or from one phone to another. You might have learnt from Physics at school that electromagnetic waves do not require a medium to propagate, they can easily pass through a vacuum, this means the Akashic record is accessible from vacuum too. Hence you will get ideas from anywhere. They travel the same way the information we send through the internet travels or from one phone to another. The only difference is that our body is the computer or here in our assumption smartphone, and the Akashic ledger is like the universe's Google. The information is stored in Akashic record using quantum memory which is the quantum-mechanical version of ordinary computer memory. Whereas ordinary memory stores information as binary states represented by 1 and 0's, quantum memory stores a quantum state for later retrieval. These states hold useful computational information known as qubits.

So now we have the internet equivalent that is Akashic records in the universe, for carrier the equivalent is waves and the smartphone is our system that is body and mind.

Essentials for successful idea generation

1. Stimulus

A boy looking out of the window of a train stimulating ideation

Now to tap into these ideas we need to need to search for these ideas in the smartphone either by using keyboard or voice/gesture search, similarly for our mind to search for information and various new ideas we need a query or stimuli, the stimuli can be internal or external too. Let us start with the external stimuli, observations what we see in our environment such as nature, architecture, people and objects can act as a stimulus. If you look through the window of a moving vehicle, you will see continuous feed of fast moving visuals this can help unlock new ideas, provided your external environment offers a diversity of scenes, a city trip will be ideal for this .Another way to stimulate visual stimuli will be to search through Google images for various keywords related to the problem that you are solving, if the problem that you are solving is related to battery, the keywords could be anything from energy storage, portable energy etc

If you engage in conversations with people, having talks or interactions with people on the topic of your interest in the field that you are seeking ideas, say for example how to prevent coconut from falling on people could be a discussion point, whether in person, over the phone, through digital means can introduce new ideas. If you are not able to converse then just reading through forums, you can use platform like Quora where people have posted similar questions, answers and discussions which can help stimulate new ideas. Just by reading through the related questions, answers and comments in forums it can give you a new direction to your ideas.

Media such as books, articles, movies, documentaries, podcasts and other form of media can expose us to new concept, designs and viewpoints. Music can be used as a trigger to activate your brain's creative potential. Music can trigger new ideas. Music can energize the brain in ways that promote flexible thinking, which can lead to innovative ideas. For example, listening to happy music with a strong emotional impact and catchy beat can increase the number of ideas, however it is true only for short exposures, continuously playing music all day doesn't contribute to any energization and in fact it may throw you out of focus from getting ideas. Also playing completing new unheard songs works better as opposed to you a playlist you have regularly, as there is nothing new in it, your brain is accustomed to it. Visual art and literature are also known to act as stimuli to generate new ideas.

Now coming back to internal stimuli, taking time to draw upon past experiences, memories, and knowledge can provide rich fodder for generating new creative ideas. Reflecting on past successes, failures, or interesting experiences can spark fresh insights and inspire innovative solutions. I personally have a repository of my past success memories and ideas, once in a while I like going through them.

Making connections between seemingly unrelated concepts or ideas can lead to novel insights. Associative thinking involves linking disparate pieces of information or concepts to generate new perspectives and ideas.

Visualization techniques, such as mentally picturing different possibilities or outcomes, can help generate new ideas and solutions. Cultivating a curious mindset and asking probing questions to oneself can pave way to new discoveries and ideas. Strong emotions, such as passion, excitement, or frustration, can drive creative thinking and problem-solving. Embracing and channelling these emotions can lead to breakthrough ideas. Trusting one's intuition and gut feelings can sometimes lead to unexpected insights and ideas. Intuition often taps into subconscious knowledge and experiences, offering a unique perspective on problems or challenges.

Also when you start practicing mindfulness and meditation, it really helps to stop thinking and make your thoughts extremely clear, this can actually make it easier to come up with fresh ideas. By being more present and noticing items more, you start seeing amazing links and patterns you didn't see before.

Detection of patterns and connecting the dots can help unlock new possibilities; by observing patterns in data, behaviour, or market trends, individuals can identify emerging opportunities or challenges. Recognizing these trends can inspire new ideas for products, services, or solutions that address evolving needs or capitalize on emerging trends.

Systems thinking involves understanding complex systems and the relationships between their components. By analysing systems and identifying patterns of interaction, individuals can uncover opportunities for innovation and develop holistic solutions that address underlying systemic issues.

By looking for similarities in things that don't seem related at first, you can get some really great ideas; the concrete and clear culmination of this is when you see the parallels and use what you learn in one area to think of spectacular items in another. Figuring out what might happen down the road or spotting trends can make you think of fresh innovative thoughts. When you pull lessons from the data or trends we have now, you can basically see into the future to come up with ways to tackle upcoming challenges or opportunities before they even happen.

Analysing recurring patterns in problems and their solutions can inspire new ideas for addressing similar challenges. By recognizing commonalities across different problems, individuals can develop innovative approaches that apply solutions from one context to solve problems in another.

Both external and internal stimuli play important role in the ideation process, they provide the raw materials our mind needs to work to get new ideas, make connections and solve problems. By actively seeking out diverse sources of stimuli yet relevant and related to the problem that we are solving and being open to new experiences we can enhance our creativity and innovation.

You may or may not agree with me in notion of downloading new ideas from the universe, the way to look at it would be, a new born baby doesn't have any knowledge or information yet. Babies are constantly thinking about how objects behave and interact with each other, and they are also gathering information about their environment and picking up patterns, so in a way they are constantly downloading new thoughts and ideas even before they are born. More clarity and clues around this can be found when we move to animal kingdom, studies have shown that baby mice can see before their eyes open, and that their developing retinas simulate vision and send informational waves. These early activities are called "dream-like" activity, and they help mice anticipate what they will experience after opening their eyes, so they can respond immediately to environmental threats.

2. Clear objective and a well-defined problem

Without a clear objective or problem statement, you might find yourself wandering aimlessly or generating ideas that don't address the core issue. You need to understand the problem you are trying to solve in detail and split or break down the problem into its basic constituents and focus one big problem that

Elon Musk took on the challenge of making rockets reusable by breaking down the problem into manageable pieces and systematically addressing each one. He first identified that the exorbitant cost of space exploration stemmed from rockets being used only once, leading to astronomical expenses for each mission. Musk then dissected the problem into key components: the high cost of manufacturing, the challenges of recovery and refurbishment, and concerns about reliability and safety with reused rockets.

To tackle the issue of manufacturing costs, Musk and his team at SpaceX focused on building rockets with reusability in mind from the start. They aimed to simplify designs and manufacturing processes to cut down on expenses. For the recovery and refurbishment aspect, SpaceX developed innovative technologies such as grid fins, landing legs, and advanced re-entry burns to enable rockets to return to Earth intact and ready for quick refurbishment. Additionally, Musk ensured that reliability was not compromised by conducting extensive testing and implementing rigorous inspection and refurbishment processes to meet the same safety standards as new rockets. Through constant iteration, testing, and refinement, SpaceX demonstrated the viability of reusable rockets with successful landings and reuse of Falcon 9 boosters, showcasing significant cost-saving potential for the aerospace industry. will make the most impact.

So as an essential for idea generation you need to have a well-defined simple fundamental problem in mind which you can remember easily.

3. Diverse Perspectives

Bullet train inspired by kingfisher's beak

Having diverse perspectives is essential for successful idea generation because it brings together a variety of viewpoints, experiences, and expertise that can lead to more innovative and comprehensive solutions. You might have seen that usually when individuals from different backgrounds, cultures, and disciplines collaborate, they bring unique insights and approaches to the table. These diverse perspectives can spark creativity, challenge assumptions, and uncover blind spots that may not have been apparent otherwise. By considering a range of viewpoints, teams can generate ideas that are more inclusive, adaptable, and reflective of the diverse needs of their audience or users. For a single individual to think from a diverse perspective the individual need to have knowledge about a variety of fields and subjects, a medical problem can be handled with a solution from mechanical engineering, similarly an engineering problem can be solved by taking up inspiration from nature.

Some of the best solutions inspired by biomimicry draw inspiration from the incredible designs and mechanisms found in nature. For example, the development of Velcro was inspired by the way burrs cling to fur, while the design of the Shinkansen bullet train's nose was influenced by the kingfisher's beak to reduce noise and increase speed. Similarly, the Lotus Effect, inspired by the water-repellent properties of lotus leaves, has led to the creation of self-cleaning surfaces in architecture and technology. Biomimicry has also inspired advancements in materials science, such as the development of lightweight, strong structures based on the principles of spider silk. These solutions demonstrate the power of nature as a source of innovation, providing sustainable and efficient solutions to human challenges.

Organizations really get ahead by embracing all sorts of diversity that means everything from race to age to where people come from. Because of this, teams get to share different wisdom and viewpoints. This isn't simply about having a large amount of ideas but also about making everyone feel like they're truly part of the team. When you don't simply stick to one way of thinking and instead look at multiple options, you get significantly better results. It is moreover apparent to us that this setup leads to being more open and more into working together: getting everyone's take on things doesn't only increase innovation but also makes a real mark in the world.

4. Mind Mapping

To be honest, I consider mind mapping extremely important if you want to come up with marvellous ideas. It's because it shows us how things connect, helps us get our thoughts in order, and lets us explore disparate manners to solve problems. Mind mapping throws all your ideas on the page in a manner that's not only straight lines and it's all about seeing everything at once and still being able to focus on the tiny details; this method is really about letting your brain go and find out where it leads you, connecting dots that you might not have thought to connect before. It's a way of thinking that's primarily focused on breaking out of the usual and coming up with fresh new ideas. In addition, when you mind map as a group, it's easier to place your ideas into the amalgam and build on what others are including the area. In the end, it helps very different ideas come together in a way that can actually make a difference. In the subsequent chapter of this book, I will cover a mind map tool that combines with AI that you can try out.

5. Prototyping and Iteration

Prototyping means you're either doodling your first ideas on a piece of paper, putting together a model from cardboard, or possibly creating the design in a 3D program such as AutoCAD, Siemens NX. By laying down your initial thoughts on paper, you spark a chain of related wisdom and get a clearer picture of where your concepts might stumble. It's not simply about having an idea it means making that idea grow and fixing any problems since creation and improvement go hand in hand. Through making a basic version or model to test out and get opinions on, one may immerse themselves in the knowledge that comes from seeing their creation take form, spotting the good parts, the not-so-good parts, and figuring out how to make it better. This cycle of making something, getting feedback, and then adjusting is known as iteration.

It's a loop of refining, based on what people say, test results, and any fresh ideas that come to mind, making your creation stronger each time around. This manner of learning fast and somewhat slightly adjusting enables ideas to morph and upgrade into more amazing versions of themselves.

Creators can push the boundaries and achieve amazing things by always thinking about how they can do better. This mindset of never stopping to improve leads to incredible, strong ideas that focus on the people using them. Since things are tested out with prototypes in actual situations or with real people, any big problems can get spotted and sorted out early. This means less wasted time and resources. There's a profound and deep-seated certainty that trying out different solutions can spark more creativity. By sticking to this manner of creating and making changes as needed, not only are risks lowered but it also keeps the door wide open for spectacular, new ideas to come through.

6. Environment

I consider a location where you can share ideas with others and not be scared of getting things wrong to be extremely important whether it is online or offline for coming up with marvellous new ideas. Consider this if you are in a situation that's all about working together and trying out new things, you are much more likely to think outside the box. Whether we are discussing a physical spot made for team work and coming up with material together, or a feeling where everyone's opinion matters and taking a leap is celebrated, it really matters. Now, the tenor of where you're at, for instance, if people are an advocate for sharing different points of view and actually trying things, it can really change what ideas come out and how people react to them.

For example, if you're somewhere that's an advocate for being open, trusting each other, and working together, you're likely to see some inventive ideas appearing. On flip, places that aren't into listening to everyone or are scared of trying things and not doing well, those places probably won't see much in the way of anything new or exciting. In short, having an environment that's all about fostering creativity, working together, and valuing everyone's input is key to coming up with ideas that really break the Mold and make a splash.

7. Cross-disciplinary Collaboration

Cross-disciplinary collaboration is the cornerstone of successful idea generation, as it brings together diverse perspectives, skills, and experiences to tackle complex problems from multiple angles. When experts from different fields collaborate, they bring unique insights that can lead to innovative solutions that may not have been possible otherwise. For example, engineers working with psychologists might develop user-friendly technology by understanding human behaviour and preferences, leading to more effective products.

Bringing people together from different fields does something really spectacular: it makes everyone think differently and come up with fresh ideas that wouldn't have been possible if everyone stuck to their own area. You may not think it but in what you may think is stark contrast, this manner of mixing expertise from everywhere is key for coming up with big, revolutionary solutions. It's not just about fixing problems better; it regards everyone learning from each other and understanding things from new angles. Truly, working across disciplines isn't simply good for creating new ideas; it's extremely important for pushing ahead with innovation and tackling the tough material no one field can handle on its own.

8. Creative Exercises

The act of thinking out ideas is also a creative exercise, it is more like mind gyms the more you practice and think out more ideas, the better ideas you can think and that to with ease and at your will.

Creative practices are extremely important for coming up with good thoughts, they're focused on pushing our minds to think differently, get over any idea slumps, and spark new, innovative thoughts; through content such as thinking up a significant number of different outcomes or viewpoints, and not only sticking with the first idea that comes to mind, these exercises get everyone to broaden their horizons. When people do things together, like sharing all their ideas in a brainstorm, without worrying about being judged, it can really get their minds working and bring up masterstroke ideas. And then there's various activities that help line up our thoughts properly, such as drawing out our ideas with mind maps or playing with words to see how they connect, which makes it significantly easier to stumble upon something amazing or figure out a fix to a problem.

For instance, if you act like you are another person through role-playing, you can understand different perspectives and come up with intelligent and informed solutions: by doing things such as creating stories or writing down ideas, you not only get amazing new ideas but also get everyone to work together better. Those activities are all about using your imagination and creativity freely, so you can discover new ways to look at everything. One may immerse themselves in the knowledge that these fun ways of brainstorming are key for creating something truly impressive and fresh.

9. Feedback and Evaluation

One clearly can envision how discussing your ideas with others can really help you make them better. You learn what is good about your idea, what needs work, and how you can improve it. Opinions and checking really matter when you're coming up with ideas because those opinions from different people add so much value; they let you see where you can make your ideas better through the months and years. You should always try to get comments on your ideas by sharing them, which leads to spotting your strengths and weaknesses; this method will always help in generating better ideas.

Whether it's constructive criticism from peers, mentors, or potential users, feedback enables creators to iterate on their ideas and make them more robust. For example, receiving feedback from customers during product development can lead to enhancements that better meet their needs and preferences, ultimately resulting in a more successful outcome.

In a group project, when everyone includes ideas in the pot, it's not simply about saying yes or no to each one. Evaluation takes those ideas, checks them out against a list of what we're supposed to achieve, and sees which ones actually make sense. By looking at how possible, impactful, and on-target each idea is, teams can figure out which sketches to dig into deeper: essentially, instead of wasting time on material that isn't going to fly or doesn't fit the plan, you already know which paths might be winners. If you're working on a design project, looking at different models and seeing how real users react can point you to the champ solution. One can see, unquestionably so, that giving feedback and rating those ideas is extremely key in getting through the storm of brainstorming to find those golden ideas that really could turn out great.

We can conduct various analysis on ideas, once such analysis is conducting a SWOT analysis for feedback on your idea, it's essential to assess the strengths, weaknesses, opportunities, and threats associated with the feedback received.

When you get feedback on your idea, it shows what's working really well and what's not. Those things that people say are great? They prove your idea has some good material worth focusing on and can boost your confidence and drive to keep going but then, there's the other part when feedback tells you where you're missing the mark or things aren't extremely clear. That's your cue to get to work on fixing those components, making your idea even better. Just think of it as doing a SWOT analysis whenever you discuss with someone about your idea and take what they say to heart. And we may thus possibly conclude, thinking scrupulously about both the good and not-so-good feedback is extremely crucial.

Moving to opportunities, feedback presents an opportunity to further develop and enhance your idea. By carefully analysing feedback, you may uncover new avenues for improvement or expansion that you hadn't considered before. This could involve refining features, targeting new markets, or exploring partnerships to strengthen your idea's overall value proposition. Finally, threats in the feedback may indicate challenges or obstacles that could impede the success of your idea if not addressed. These could include competitors with similar offerings, potential market risks, or technological limitations that need to be overcome.

Summing it all up, by doing a SWOT analysis on feedback about your idea, you get to make the most of what's strong about it, repair the weak spots, take advantage of opportunities that come your way, and get rid of anything dangerous; this way, it guides you to improve and make your idea much stronger so it does much better. It is moreover apparent to you and that this will help our ideas a lot.

10. *Continuous Learning and Curiosity*

Continuous learning and curiosity are indispensable for successful idea generation as they fuel exploration, innovation, and adaptation to change. In a rapidly evolving world, staying curious and committed to learning enables individuals to keep up with emerging trends, technologies, and insights across various domains. By continuously expanding their knowledge base, individuals are better equipped to identify new opportunities, connect disparate ideas, and think creatively. For instance, a software developer who stays curious about advancements in artificial intelligence may discover novel ways to integrate AI into their projects, leading to innovative solutions that meet evolving market demands.

You may be curious about how always learning and asking questions help people come up with brand-new ideas, when people keep learning new material, they get better at tackling tough challenges, making mistakes without giving up, and looking for new ideas; this positive attitude helps them stay alert and get past any obstacles that come their way when they're trying to think of something innovative. Being curious gets people to look for different answers, ask several questions, and try items that are out of the box; this can lead groups and whole companies to be more creative together. If companies really push for people to be curious, they make a location where everyone's excited to dive deep, take chances, and stretch the limits. Keeping the learning fun and curious are extremely important if you want to be great at coming up with next-level ideas because they help everyone adapt, get creative, and do really well in a world that keeps changing: people who work somewhere that encourage curiosity and keeps learning going can bring all their brainpower together to cook up revolutionary ideas that help their company stand out and grow.

11. Constraints as Catalysts

Embracing constraints as catalysts for creativity can significantly aid in idea generation by prompting innovative thinking and pushing teams to find unconventional solutions. When faced with limitations such as budget, time, or resources, teams are forced to think outside the box and explore alternative approaches. Rather than seeing constraints as barriers, encouraging the team to view them as creative challenges can spark new ideas and solutions that might not have been considered otherwise. For example, some of the most frugal ideas that I have ever thought out was by having the constraints in mind during the idea generation stage itself, if we have a small budget for the solution of the problem this can encourage us to think more innovatively and help eliminate all expensive solutions, a limited budget might inspire the team to find more cost-effective materials or processes, while a tight deadline could lead to streamlined workflows and innovative problem-solving methods. By embracing constraints, teams can unlock their creativity and produce ideas that are both inventive and practical, ultimately leading to more successful outcomes.

CHAPTER II

How to Think Out Jugaad or Frugal Ideas & How to Combine Human and Artificial Intelligence

Jugaad is a Hindi word that roughly translates to "innovative hack" or "workaround." It refers to finding quick, makeshift solutions using limited resources. Jugaad is often associated with resourcefulness, creativity, and making things work with what's available. It's a common practice in many parts of the world, especially in developing countries, where people face constraints in terms of finances, infrastructure, or technology.

Similarly, "frugal" refers to being economical or thrifty, making the most of limited resources. In the context of problem-solving or innovation, frugal solutions involve achieving the desired outcome with minimal expense or waste. Frugal innovation often focuses on simplicity, efficiency, and sustainability. It's about finding ways to do more with less.

Both jugaad and frugal innovation emphasize the importance of being resourceful and creative in finding solutions to problems, particularly when faced with constraints such as limited funds, materials, or infrastructure.

To think out Jugaad ideas we should first set out constraints, this would include listing down all the available resources or pre deciding the budget. You can think it more in terms of a food recipe, we first list out all the elements we have with us in the kitchen and then prepare a recipe utilizing the available resources in the best possible ways meeting the various constraints.

We should Look for existing solutions, both locally and globally, that address similar problems. Analyse what works and what doesn't, and consider how you can adapt or improve upon existing ideas. We should Engage with communities and individuals who are known for their innovative practices, whether it's through networking events, online forums, or social media groups. Learn from their experiences and insights.

Don't be afraid to experiment with different ideas and prototypes. Start small, test your concepts, and iterate based on feedback and results. We should Consider the environmental impact of your jugaad solutions and aim for sustainability. Look for ways to minimize waste, use renewable resources, and create long-lasting solutions. Open Source Communities and DIY Portal like Instructables help us discover many hacks and jugaad from people around the world which will serve as inspiration and we can build and improvise them. Engage with open-source communities and platforms where people share ideas, projects, and solutions freely.

In India, people face all sorts of difficulties, such as being short on many things while having many people living there, due to these problems, it's pretty important for them to use whatever they've got in as many ways as possible. I believe, as you might hold credence also, that this need turns into something cool - thinking of clever solutions - it's basically being extremely intelligent and informed with what you have; they get extremely creative in using items and material in little yet clever ways to save money and work around what's limited, this notion has a lot to do with just how diverse India is, from city to city, there's an array of different problems people experience which rather pushes everyone to come up with smart ideas, there's even a large push for people to just solve problems by themselves without waiting for anyone to fix it for them, which is part of the reason why so many in India are good at inventing items and just experimenting with things until they work. I guess, growing up surrounded by different challenges primes you to rather always be in a state of finding workarounds, which is pretty impressive.

Cultivating a habit of resourcefulness starts from home, if something breaks down in your house which can be easily fixed by you, then if you are a person who needs a mechanic to fix it then you are in fact less resourceful, on the other hand if you are someone who could find a repair manual online and fix it, you are resourceful, when you make this a habit you will accumulate lot of knowledge that would help you think different and Jugaad.

To truly understand the essence of Jugaad innovation, one must appreciate the role of improvisation in everyday life. It's about leveraging what's immediately available and reimagining its use to solve problems creatively. Imagine a rural mechanic fixing a broken-down vehicle with basic tools and scrap materials, this showcases the ingenuity that lies at the heart of Jugaad. This resourcefulness can be harnessed in various fields, from engineering to everyday household fixes, encouraging a mindset that sees potential solutions in unexpected places.

The idea that being nimble in innovation is of the very highest importance gets spotlighted by the fact that operations can keep going nicely even when things outside get rough, turning to a different strategy in reaction to changes in the market, without having to spend a substantial amount of extra money, is what being good at Jugaad can mean for a business. Let's say there's a problem in the supply chain, a firm could change what their machines make to put out items people really want today. When the world brings surprises, the capacity to change things and not simply stick to the old plan is of significant consequence, there can possibly be gratification in your knowing that this flexibility is an intelligent and informed move for staying ahead.

Within the concentrated environment, or world of technology, creating straightforward but meaningful tools that target unique local requirements is made possible through Jugaad. Take, for example, the crafting of mobile apps tailored for places where the internet is barely there. Such apps don't take up much data or need a significant quotient of power to run but they're extremely important because they let people use items such as bank services, learning content, and health care. They really zero in on what's really needed, cutting out all the material that's not needed, which makes them extremely usable and reachable for the people they're made for. One, if they so choose, may ponder how concentrating on just the important parts helps the apps to better serve their purpose.

Teachers in schools that don't have a significant quotient of resources could get creative by turning items such as bottle caps into counting tools for math. This way, children don't only learn their numbers they also see how important it is to be inventive and flexible. By pushing for this somewhat innovative thinking, we could help raise several students who understand how to tackle problems in new ways. We hope this piece may teach and show how much Jugaad innovation can change learning.

Jugaad's emphasis on sustainability aligns perfectly with the growing global focus on environmental conservation. Innovations born from this mindset often incorporate eco-friendly practices, such as using biodegradable materials or designing products that require less energy to produce and operate. By integrating sustainability into the core of innovation processes, Jugaad not only addresses immediate problems but also contributes to long-term ecological balance, ensuring that solutions are both effective and responsible.

Items made using discarded coconut shell

Yet another great way to inculcate Jugaad skills would be to repurpose the waste in your house, by doing this you are becoming more resourceful, I know this is a small thing but these are small steps in the right direction, which would eventually help think out revolutionary Jugaad innovations. Even think out different crafts that you can make out of coconut shell would exercise your brain to think out more innovative ideas.

For example, thinking about innovative uses for coconut shells is akin to a mental workout that strengthens your creativity and problem-solving skills. Just as lifting weights builds muscle, engaging in ideation exercises hones your ability to think outside the box and develop unique solutions. Each time you brainstorm new crafts or practical applications for coconut shells, you are essentially flexing your mental muscles, making them stronger and more capable of generating high-quality ideas in various contexts.

Crowdsourcing ideas can be compared to participating in a group fitness class. When you engage with a community to share and develop ideas, you benefit from the diverse perspectives and experiences of others. This collaborative environment fosters a collective creativity that surpasses what any single individual might achieve alone. Much like how group exercises can push you to new limits and improve your overall fitness, crowdsourcing can enhance the quality and originality of your ideas through the synergistic effect of multiple minds working together.

Regularly practicing ideation is essential for maintaining and improving your creative fitness. Just as consistency is key in a physical workout regimen, routinely challenging yourself to think of new uses for everyday items like coconut shells ensures that your creative faculties remain sharp and agile. Over time, this practice not only boosts your ability to come up with innovative solutions quickly but also increases the variety and sophistication of the ideas you generate. Like building endurance through repeated exercise, sustained mental effort strengthens your capacity for sustained creative thinking.

The process of developing ideas from coconut shells into actual crafts mirrors the progression of a fitness journey. Initially, you might start with simple projects, such as turning a coconut shell into a bowl or a decorative piece. As you gain more experience and confidence, you can tackle more complex creations, like intricate jewellery or functional household items. This progression reflects how beginners might start with basic exercises and gradually move on to more advanced routines, continually challenging themselves to achieve greater levels of creativity and skill.

Ultimately, the analogy between creative thinking and physical exercise highlights the importance of persistence and effort in both areas. Just as a gym-goer might set fitness goals and track their progress, those engaged in ideation should set creativity goals and reflect on their development over time. By viewing your brain as a muscle that needs regular, varied, and challenging workouts, you can foster a mindset that embraces continuous improvement and innovation. Whether you're brainstorming new uses for coconut shells or solving more complex problems, this approach ensures that your creative abilities are always growing stronger and more versatile.

Jugaad innovation is a powerful concept that goes beyond mere problem-solving. It fosters a culture of ingenuity, adaptability and sustainability, providing a framework for creating impactful solutions with limited resources. By embracing this philosophy, individuals and organizations can navigate challenges more effectively, leading to innovations that are both practical and transformative.

When you get your hands dirty building something from the ground up, experimenting with different items, or even fixing a stuck tool, it really kicks your creativity and cleverness into high gear; this type of hands-on work makes you deal with limits upfront, which really teaches you to come up with fixes on the fly, using items you have just sitting around. Experimenting with tools and supplies give you fresh, unexpected wisdom and methods that just thinking about material in your head wouldn't. Fiddling around with physical things is inherently similar to fueling your brain to come up with new ideas in a way that book-learning doesn't always quite hit the mark.

Teaming up for group projects can really open the door to amazing creative ideas. When you work with people who have all sorts of different skills and come from various backgrounds, you get to see things from several new angles. This path to discovery and discernment is all about mixing different thoughts and methods together, which is extremely wonderful because sometimes one weird idea from someone can create a new answer for somebody else. Places like brainstorming get-togethers, workshops, and maker spaces are perfect spots for this essentially teamwork. They're not only about everyone including their components of knowledge, they also set up this fun place where imaginative fixes can grow thanks to everyone joining forces and getting creative.

Volunteering for community projects, heading out to places where items aren't easy to find or just trying out your own frugal projects can really help you think of new ideas. Engaging with real-life issues teaches outcomes. Facing these situations makes us get creative on the spot because we must. Experimenting with what you can make and seeing how others deal with the same essential challenges, you get pretty sharp at coming up with marvellous solutions. It is clearly apparent to you and I that working with real problems boosts how flexible and very creative you can be in solving things, this way of learning shows you how to find opportunities where others only see obstacles, turning difficulties into starting points for smart and informed solutions.

It may have once seemed unfathomable but we know that creating new things while working can actually solve some pretty big problems with very little. Think about a farmer in the countryside of India. He must water his fields but he's got no special equipment to do it. What is his job? He takes whatever he can find, old bicycle components, plastic bottles, and thrown-out hoses and puts together this homemade water pump. It is a very simple setup but it works. The farmer's crops get the water they need. This just goes to show that you don't need all the high-technology gadgets to come up with solutions. Sometimes, you just need to work with what you have, and that's at the heart of being able to improvise.

In a farming area where people mostly grow food, a spectacular sort of scarecrow with springs does significantly more than you'd think for a farmer's life, most of the time, the antiquated scarecrows don't cut it because birds and other critters become accustomed to them and are not frightened anymore. But, if a farmer figures out how to put springs in a scarecrow, the thing starts moving in a significant quotient of weird ways, especially when the wind blows or something bumps into it. Almost inevitably, we open, this ends up working a lot better because the constant movement scares the animals, so they stay away from the crops. And, it's of significant consequence, not simply for keeping the food plants safe. When pests don't eat all their material, farmers and their families have more food and money. Less food getting snatched by animals means they can sell more, eat well, and they don't have to worry as much about cash, this is extremely important because how well the harvest goes essentially decides whether they're having a good year or struggling. With enough food and more money from a solid harvest, families can live healthier, maybe even focus on learning more or repairing the home, showing how one intelligent and informed move with a scarecrow can actually help in many ways.

So, this extremely intelligent and informed scarecrow isn't simply about scaring birds away, it's of significant consequence because it can save people by cutting down on the need for dangerous pest-killing chemicals. Usually, if farmers don't have a better way to keep bugs off their crops, they think they must use these nasty chemicals, even though they know it could be bad for their health. With this wonderful, mechanical solution that works perfectly and doesn't need anything but just a spring to work, farmers don't have to use those harmful substances. This means not simply the farmer but his family and all the nature around them are a lot safer. In a very basic essence, a new, simple scarecrow is all about making lives better, protecting health, and showing that sometimes the best way to solve an enormous problem is to use new ideas.

In urban settings, improvisation through Jugaad can be seen in the way people tackle everyday challenges. For instance, street vendors in crowded cities often face the issue of transporting their goods efficiently. Without the means to afford expensive transport equipment, many turn to modifying their bicycles or creating pushcarts from reclaimed wood and wheels. These improvised solutions not only help them move their goods but also adapt to the narrow, congested streets of the city. By thinking creatively and adapting on the fly, these vendors demonstrate the practicality and effectiveness of Jugaad.

Improvisation in Jugaad is not limited to physical creations but extends to processes and services as well.

The COVID-19 pandemic made everyone see how intelligent and informed and flexible people can be when they're facing a really tough situation. Suddenly, we had to deal with not having enough masks and face shields because of an enormous shortage of personal protective equipment (PPE). Since it was extremely hard to find professional-grade PPE, people everywhere started to make their own out of things they had lying around, such as pieces of fabric, plastic sheets, or by using 3D printers. It was really great because everyone was pitching in to make these homemade masks and shields, which was a way for us all to help protect ourselves and the people around us, the concrete and clear culmination of this was when these DIY fixes began appearing all over, showing us that when we come together and think on our feet, we can find quick and effective ways to fix some serious problems.

Engineers and innovators took on an enormous challenge when hospitals everywhere started running out of ventilators for treating serious COVID-19 patients. In countries such as India, groups of young engineers and health experts got together to build improvised ventilators out of things they could easily find, like Ambu bags, motors, and simple tubes. Even though these DIY ventilators weren't as good as the ones you buy, they were extremely important for helping patients in places where there's not a significant quotient of resources, this just goes to show, we can take as a definite certainty that when people really need to solve a problem because they don't have what they usually would, they come up with some really creative ideas. Developing low-cost ventilators and other medical gadgets was a major intelligent and informed move.

Healthcare providers in both rural and urban areas started using basic mobile phones and apps like WhatsApp to speak to patients remotely, this idea, called Jugaad, meant people could get help and advice from doctors without having to go see them, which was very good for keeping the virus from spreading. Because of the pandemic, people also came up with the intelligent and informed idea to use remote healthcare and online learning, especially where it was hard to get to see a doctor in person before: one mustn't deny that these smart actions were all about making the best out of a tough situation, to make sure people who had to isolate could do it safely, people in the local area and local groups got schools, community halls, and even tents to serve as temporary isolation spots, this situation showed how an interesting combination of local knowledge and extremely simple technology could really step up to help out during the extremely difficult time of a global health emergency. It's a perfect example of Jugaad, using what you have in clever ways to fix big problems, proving exactly how making quick and intelligent and informed changes can actually save lives.

India has a rich cultural heritage with a long history of innovation and invention in various fields such as mathematics, science, medicine, and technology. This legacy of innovation continues to influence modern-day problem-solving approaches.

Previously, way back around 600 BCE, there was Sushruta living in India. He was extremely important because he essentially kick-started the whole surgery and medicine in India, this person wrote down all his genius thoughts and discoveries in the Sushruta Samhita, which is a very old book describing how to do surgery and help people heal. Among the spectacular ideas he figured out, there's one thing that amazes me, he actually used ants to stitch up cuts. You heard it correctly ants! Why ants of all things, Sushruta was onto something because these weren't only any ants but big black ones with strong jaws. He was using the ants' mandibles to pinch the edges of wounds together, which is pretty clever when you think about it. You will feel better when you understand that this method wasn't only about holding the wound closed. He knew these ant bites could help because they also made the wound clean, acting like nature's own antiseptic. That way, the risk of infections was reduced, which is of significant consequence when you're doing surgery. It is moreover apparent to you and me that this was some next-level thinking.

Using ants as a natural stitch-up kit not only shows how perceptive early Indian doctors like Sushruta were but also their ability to make the most of what nature offered. Even though it sounds outlandish to us now, it was a very important new idea back then. This is definitely a reminder of how advancements in medical technology really hinge on observation and ingenuity, drawing upon the very world around us.

Farmers in Southeast Asia found a clever way with bamboo to water their plants. They took bamboo sticks, made holes in them, and let water drip slowly to their crop fields. It's a simple way to make sure their plants get just the right amount of water without too much hassle. Then there's a method from ancient India for cleaning water, thought up by Charaka. He suggested filtering water with sand, gravel, and charcoal, which might sound very simple now, but at that time, Charaka Samhita was a clever method to make drinking water safer. A discerning reader may begin to register how people in ancient Egypt were also very smart. They mixed mud, sand, and straw to create a mortar. This wasn't only a simple mixture, it was what they used to build those large pyramids that don't get knocked down by the weather or time. Moving on to something more recent but still impressive, there's the Jaipur Foot. In India, some smart people designed it to help those who've lost their legs. It's made of rubber, wood, and aluminium, which might not sound special but it's inexpensive, works well, and lasts a long time: this has been revolutionary, especially for those living in the countryside where money for high-technology prosthetics isn't really a thing.

Finally, there's the Mitticool fridge made by Mansukhbhai Prajapati in Gujarat, this is not like the usual things you find in a kitchen. It's built out of clay and doesn't need any electricity to work. It keeps food nice and tasty through evaporative cooling, which is of significant consequence in places that are both hot and dry. Contextually, each of these innovations, from different times and places, shows how creative humans have always been when solving everyday problems.

During the COVID-19 pandemic, SpiceJet, an Indian airline, repurposed its passenger aircraft to carry cargo in the passenger seats. This frugal innovation helped the airline generate revenue while passenger travel was restricted, utilizing existing infrastructure in a new way.

Dabbawala Lunchbox Delivery is another such example of frugal innovation in logistics, Mumbai's dabbawalas are known for their efficient and low-cost lunchbox delivery service. Using bicycles and trains, they deliver home-cooked meals from people's homes to their workplaces with remarkable accuracy, relying on a simple yet effective coding system.

Jugaad ideas are basically about being extremely resourceful, finding intelligent and informed ways to solve problems without needing a large amount of new or pricey material, they're about keeping things really simple and not making them more complicated than they have to be, the whole idea is to use what you have already to its fullest, turning frugality into a way to get things done. By focusing on getting the job done with minimal resources, everybody can actually afford these solutions, making it significantly easier for more people to benefit from them.

Since these solutions are meant to be put together quickly, thinking fast and finding quick solutions is a key part of the process.

In addition, they're not only famous for just one thing. Jugaad solutions can be adjusted or changed to sort out new issues as they come up. What really matters is that these ideas work for the people using them, tackling real matters directly and effectively, all without costing too much money, this manner of problem-solving is a journey on the path to discovery and discernment, keeping it cleverly simple and straight to the point. It fits when the goals are more about the goals we need to hit today, and not about having everything polished and picture-perfect.

Creativity and risk-taking are also integral to Jugaad. Innovators often employ a high level of creativity and out-of-the-box thinking, coming up with unconventional solutions that might not be immediately obvious. Since Jugaad frequently involves trying out untested or unconventional methods, it includes an element of risk-taking and experimentation. Overall, Jugaad embodies a blend of practicality, creativity, and resourcefulness, making it a powerful approach to problem-solving, especially in resource-constrained environments.

Do you think you understand Jugaad now based on what I have explained, so let me give you a challenge, you can use Jugaad to think out solutions.

Preventing animal accidents on railway tracks is a pressing issue, particularly in regions where wildlife habitats intersect with railways, the conventional approach putting fencing or barricades along the length of railway track is not economically feasible, let me put some math here so that you understand the value of Jugaad, the estimated budget for installing fencing along the entire railway network in India would be substantial, at around INR 50,526 crores ($606 million USD), maintaining it would be another challenge again.

One possible Jugaad solution would be Imagine a train equipped with this high-frequency system approaching a dense forest area known for frequent animal crossings. As the train nears, the system activates, sending out high-frequency waves that travel through the tracks and create a deterrent zone. Animals, sensing the approaching train through the sound and vibrations, move away from the tracks, ensuring a safe passage for both the wildlife and the train.

• • •

How to combine human and artificial intelligence?

A boy and a robot trying to combine their intelligence

Firstly a word of caution, most of the innovation challenge platforms are completely against AI driven ideas and you risk getting disqualified if you directly copy paste content from ChatGPT like tools. So this brings an important question to us, how can we use AI tool to think out better ideas?

Let me list how AI Tools like ChatGPT can help you think out more innovative ideas.

1. Existing ideas, ChatGPT can help you list existing solution and ideas, this means these are the ones that is already existing in

the market and most probably the organizer would be aware of these ideas and if you submit these ideas, you may not win the challenge.

2. Generate inspirations or stimulate thoughts with text, just by asking Chatgpt relevant and thought-provoking questions can generate textual stimulus that can trigger your mind to think out new ideas.

3. Use AI image generation tool to describe your image in words, this will help you visualize your idea and when you visualize your idea then you will be able to give better clarity to your idea and address the other challenges that could occur due to your idea and explain solutions to prevent negative points in your idea.

4. Clearly explain the problem statements, constraints and your solution, now ask ChatGPT to list various advantages and disadvantages of your idea. This way you will be able to easily identify the flaws in your solution, in your solution itself you should address the various flaws, the advantages of the solution can also be emphasized if you know the advantages.

5. You can pick famous innovators based on the field of your interest and ask ChatGPt to criticize, evaluate your idea as if you were that personality, that is for an idea in technology you can ask ChatGpt to criticize, evaluate it as if you were Steve jobs, in this case your solution will be evaluated based on core principles of Apple like principles of simplicity, elegance, and human-centric design.

6. Help come with KPI metrics, if you pass on large documents and research papers ChatGPT or similar AI tools can read and understand the data in few seconds and pull out information that is relevant to your idea and help you come up with KPI and metrics for your idea, which will show the impact of your solution, the cost savings, the cost of developing the solution and all.

7. Prediction and simulation of your ideas, you can ask ChatGPT, questions like if your product is getting used by a particular

persona of people that is say kids of age group between 10-16 in Asia, what are the problems and challenges they will encounter when using your product and anticipate the challenges and better address it to make your solution more robust.

8. Patent drafting assistance is another scope of ChatGPT like tools which can help significantly lower the time required to patent your solution and help reduce hefty cost of attorney fees.

9. You can think out many ideas and develop a rating or evaluation model that closely represents the final evaluation criteria setup for each challenge, in many challenges the judge's evaluation criteria is mentioned, so by evaluating your ideas based on the same criteria you can identify the ideas with potential and help focus your energy on those submissions.

Now let us assume that you are the solution seeker or the company organizing the innovation challenge, then there are various things you can use AI to improve the quality of innovation ideas that you get out of the crowdsourcing challenge, I will list few of them.

1. AI can automatically screen and filter submitted ideas based on predefined criteria such as feasibility, novelty, and alignment with the challenge objectives. This reduces the manual effort required by solution seekers and ensures that only relevant ideas are considered. Also, when people submit an idea to an innovation challenge they look at existing ideas and if the existing ideas is off track then the subsequent submission can also go off track hence it is important to screen ideas and make sure it meets the challenge objectives and I think AI can play certainly a big role here.

2. I have seen many big companies conducting innovation challenges with a generic objective like "How will you improve the mobility of the future", the purpose of these challenges is to understand the consumer trends and pain points, AI-powered NLP tools can analyse the content of the submitted ideas to

extract key insights, identify trends and evaluate the quality of the proposals. This helps solution seekers gain a deeper understanding of the ideas and make more informed decisions.

3. AI can perform sentiment analysis on the comments, feedback and reactions received for each idea. This way the R&D department of various companies can gauge the interest of various ideas from the community itself and focus on project where they see interest. This helps solution seekers gauge the overall sentiment towards specific ideas and identify potential areas for improvement or further exploration.

4. People submitting similar ideas is big problem in various crowdsourcing challenges and also a source of conflict in the community, usually the person who submits the idea first is rewarded. AI algorithms can cluster similar ideas together and categorize them based on their themes or features. This enables solution seekers to better organize and manage the large volume of submissions, making it easier to identify patterns and trends. Also, before the participant clicks the submit button the similar ideas can be shown which will help eliminate duplication of ideas.

5. AI can assist in detecting intellectual property (IP) infringement and plagiarism by comparing submitted ideas against existing patents, publications, and databases. This helps solution seekers protect the integrity of the innovation challenge and ensure originality.

• • •

What are the new AI Tools in the market that can help me with crowdsourcing and thinking out innovative ideas?

At the time of writing this book in 2024, I can suggest what is relevant and available and none of them are promoted by any means, these tools should serve as examples and for some reason these tools are not available in the year when you are reading this book, I would rely on you to think out similar alternatives in the market.

1. Albus is a brand new way to engage with AI technologies. Albus can breakdown topics, create insights, generate images and audio. Here is a brief description of the tool from the creator themselves.

"Albus is an AI-powered platform to take the load off them so they can wire ideas instead of shuttling between tabs and apps.

Thanks to large language models and machine learning services, a well-designed experience could surface relations and connections within a context by momentarily processing a vast amount of information, acting as a mind companion on a screen (for now). This saves precious time and attention and allows you to spark new ideas."

Now let me tell you how we can use it for thinking out better ideas, in this tool you can input any thing which is related to any problem in an innovation challenge, let us say Colgate is looking for ways to bring innovation in their tooth brush, so to start with you can put in Tooth brush.

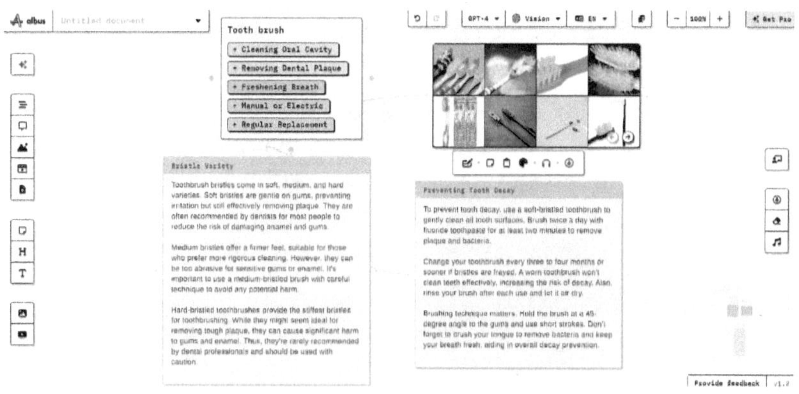

Using a mind map tool to break down 'Tooth brush'

So it will break down the tooth brush into various related items like cleaning oral cavity, removing dental plaque, freshening breath, manual or electric tooth brush, regular replacement.

When I expand on various related concepts I get more details, which triggers more ideas, if I want to visually see bristle variety, I just had to click on the image generation, the AI has created various kinds of bristle variety to give me better understanding of the topic. This tool allows me to choose various LLM models from the top.

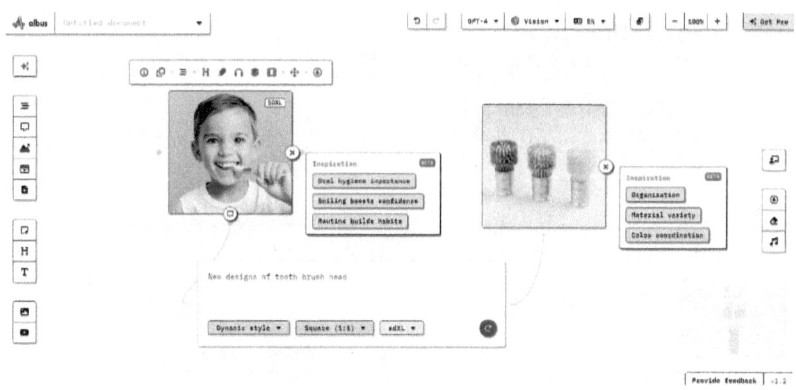

Using mind map tool to explore related concepts

Here as you can see I have asked for new designs for tooth brush head, the tool has visualized images of the new design and it also let me know the inspiration for the design, from an user point of view I also know what is important for a customer, that is oral hygiene importance, smiling boosts confidence, routine builds habits.

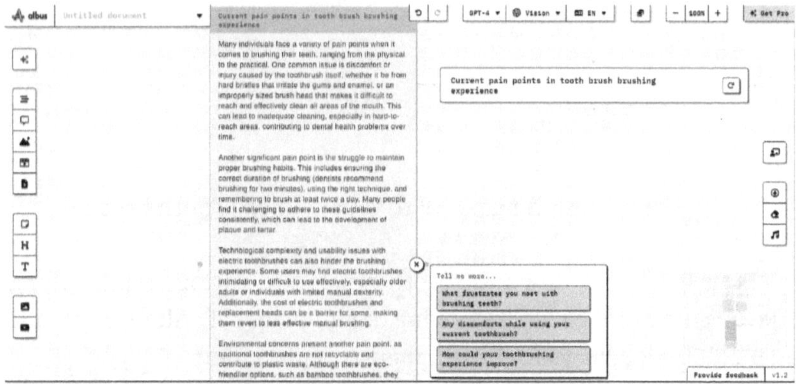

Using mind map tool to unlock hidden insights

As you can see below, I have gone ahead and asked questions like, what are the pain points in tooth brushing experience, the tool has also generated related thought provoking questions too which will serve as stimuli.

The idea board help you in asking various thought provoking questions related to the problem that you are solving that will eventually help in coming up with a robust solution for the problem and you will also be able to research the existing innovation in this domain and come up with something which is completely new to the market and that appeal to the audience.

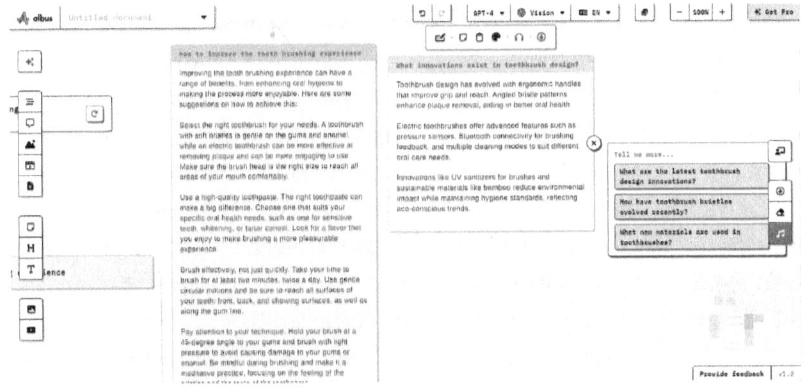

Using mind map tool question everything

2. Answer Socrates

Using this tool user can discover the questions people are asking on Google about almost any topic, for free. Answer Socrates is a powerful technique that can be effectively utilized in the ideation process. Rooted in the Socratic method of questioning, it encourages critical thinking and exploration of ideas by posing a series of questions. In ideation, this approach can be employed to dissect problems, challenge assumptions, and stimulate innovative solutions. By asking "Why?" repeatedly, participants can delve deeper into the root causes of a problem, uncovering hidden issues or perspectives that may not have been apparent initially. This method not only helps in understanding the problem comprehensively but also opens up new avenues for creative problem-solving.

Moreover, Answer Socrates can facilitate brainstorming sessions by guiding participants to think from different angles. By asking questions like "What if?" or "How might we?", it encourages divergent thinking and generates a wide range of ideas. This technique promotes a more inclusive ideation process, where everyone's perspectives are valued, leading to more diverse and potentially groundbreaking solutions. Additionally, Answer Socrates fosters a culture of curiosity and exploration within a team, encouraging them to continuously question and refine their ideas until they reach the most effective solutions. Overall, integrating Answer Socrates into the ideation process can help teams to approach problems more critically, generate innovative ideas, and ultimately drive impactful outcomes.

Using this tool user just need to put a topic and all the relevant though provoking questions based on actual user experience is obtained which can be very useful in thinking out solutions to the problem.

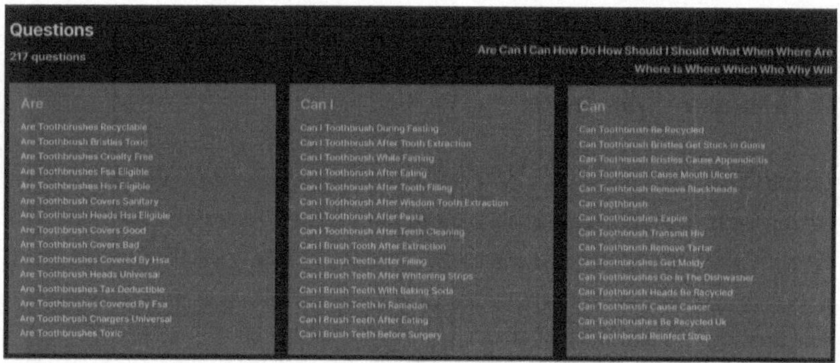

Answer socrates questions part 1

Now let me put the same topic I discussed earlier 'Tooth brush'.

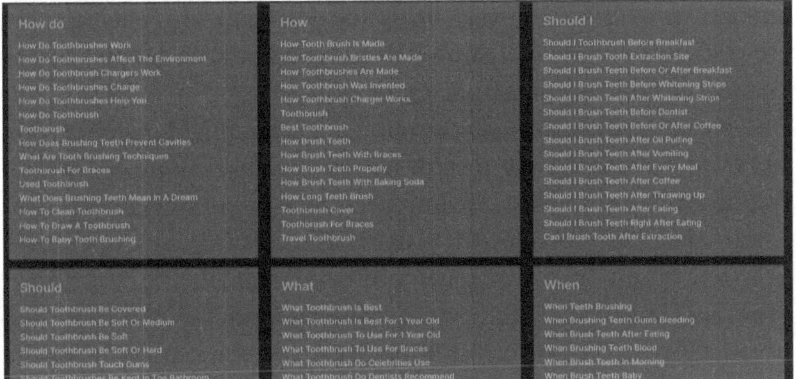

Answer socrates questions part 2

If you observe closely there are many interesting questions that can act as stimuli for you think more innovative solutions, like can tooth brush bristles get stuck in gums, can swallowing bristles cause appendicitis, there is good number of questions around recyclability of tooth brush. Below you can see more questions, I wanted to give you a feel of the questions.

3. Whimsical Mind map using AI

How about an AI-powered mind mapping tool that feels like exploring a magical forest of ideas? Picture this: you start with a blank canvas, which is like a tranquil glade. As you add your ideas, branches and leaves sprout, forming interconnected paths, like vines weaving through the trees.

Each idea you add is like planting a seed. The AI nurtures it, suggesting related concepts that blossom into colourful flowers, creating a beautiful tapestry of thoughts. You can wander through this forest, discovering new connections, and the AI acts as your guide, illuminating hidden paths and suggesting new areas to explore.

The interface could be whimsical and intuitive, with charming animations and sounds that bring the forest to life. Maybe there are friendly woodland creatures that pop up to offer helpful tips or encouragement as you map out your ideas.

As you navigate through the mind map, you might stumble upon secret groves filled with inspiration, or stumble upon a whimsical treasure trove of tools and features to enhance your creativity.

And just like a real forest, your mind map can evolve over time. You can return to it whenever you need, watching as your ideas grow and flourish like the ever-expanding branches of a tree. This is exactly what Whimsical as a too does, you can type in what you are planning to imagine and the AI will create a mind map and you can generate many related ideas which will help you ideate better. Let us examine it with the Tooth brush case.

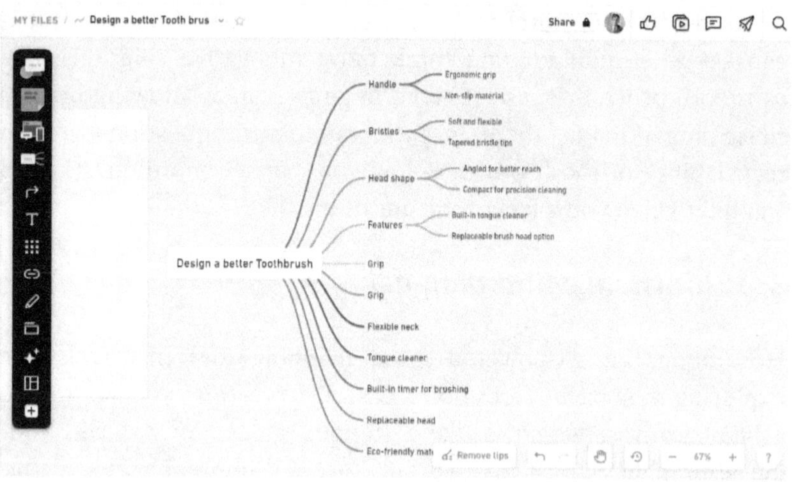

A screenshot from a mind map tool to break down tooth brush

CHAPTER III

How to Find Innovation and Crowdsourcing Challenges

There are thousands of innovation opportunities across the world, however finding them can be difficult as it is spread across the world, there are innovation challenges like Xprize that offers a staggering $ 101 Million for a single innovation challenge.

Few years ago when I was looking for various innovation opportunities I used to scan various internet sources and search the entire internet for various opportunities that is of interest to me, I understood the challenge faced by innovators in finding innovation opportunities, that is why I have started Givemechallenge.com so that users can just go to this portal which is like an aggregator of all innovation challenges across the world, top crowdsourcing and innovation portals sends us information about innovation opportunities and we list it in the portal for free and also offer promotion of these innovation challenges for a small fee which we use to run and maintain the platform.

The platform also have a Youtube channel that offers shorts videos of various innovation opportunities, users also have been provided the option of getting these opportunities through dedicated android and IOS apps.

I started this portal with a vision of making innovation opportunities accessible to the masses so that anyone across the world can easily identify various innovation opportunities by category without the need for digging the web, I was decently rewarded for starting this opportunities aggregator portal as I used to get firsthand information about any innovation opportunity across the world or even before the challenge launches, in my initial days I used to post and list close to 40 opportunities a day, this way I was aware of all the innovation opportunities around the globe, I also used to work on the relevant challenges that are of interest to me and which I think I can solve. By posting about these challenges, I get accustomed with the winning entries the rewards structure of thousands of innovation challenges, I will share my insights from experience of posting thousands of innovation opportunities in the subsequent sections.

Innovation thrives on collaboration and diverse perspectives. crowdsourcing enables access to a global pool of talent and expertise, making it a valuable tool for generating innovative solutions. Whether it's through open innovation challenges, hackathons or online platforms, crowdsourcing allows organizations to tap into the collective intelligence of the crowd and uncover novel ideas and approaches.

I can list you here the names of hundreds of innovation portals here but I am not doing that because along with this book I will be focusing on having a complete updated database of all updated innovation opportunities in my portal Givemechallenge.com, it is been around since 2015 but is not well known to many as we never focused on marketing it, still many prominent innovation portals and challenges reach out to us first when they have an innovation competition.

Givemechallenge curates and lists various challenges, competitions, contests, hackathons, scholarships, and grants from around the world. The website serves as a comprehensive resource for individuals looking to participate in a wide range of opportunities, from academic and professional contests to innovation and creativity challenges.

This platform isn't simply about random competitions there is a profound and deep-seated certainty that it is definitely a key resource for uncovering scholarships and grants for both students and working professionals. It clearly lay out all the details you need to know, like what it takes to apply, how much money you could get, and who's actually allowed to try and join. Sticking to technology, design, science, business, and social impact, the site showcases a large mix of challenges. For each one, you get all the details on items such as eligibility, when you need to submit by, what you could win, and the steps to get involved. And it doesn't stop there the site's big on putting the spotlight on new ideas and creative contests. We encourage people to come up with new technology ideas, whether that's for software, hardware, or any other sort of technology project.

Many corporates now conduct hackathons to recruit talent to the companies unlike traditional interviews this is very effective as the people work and solve a real-life problem for the company in this way the solver gets to know a firsthand experience of kinds of problems they have to solve and the seeker or the company also knows the kind of the talent they are onboarding with the new resource.

Going for a career in innovation consulting can be extremely spectacular if you start by entering into creativity and innovation contests. It's a grand path to discovery and discernment. You're in real life scenarios and situations where you have to come up with workable solutions for issues that big companies throw at you. It's not simply about being intelligent and informed these places make you use your imagination and push you to figure things out on-the-spot. And you get to work with several other people, which is amazing because it means you get better at speaking and working well with others, things you definitely need if you're aiming to get a job in consulting. Once you've cracked a few tough nuts and demonstrated your problem-solving magic and you have proved how you can stay calm under very stressful deadlines, it's a good time to hunt down those jobs in innovation consulting. In addition, all those challenges sharpen up your brain for critical thinking and coming up with out-of-the-box ideas.

You may be a little doubtful that these people known as innovation consultants are extremely important in making companies get better and do amazing activities. What they do first is closely examine what the company is doing today, they look at everything from what the company makes to how they sell items and who buys it, they're trying to figure out where the company can get better or do new things, they spend a significant amount of time looking at what other businesses are doing and what customers are fond of, so they know what changes could make an enormous difference. By focusing on these components, they point out where a company can make big differences and start doing things in a new way, these innovation consultants are noticeably focused on pushing creativity and coming up with intelligent and informed plans to help businesses stand out and grow in today's extremely complicated concentrated environment, or world of business.

Once opportunities are identified, innovation consultants develop tailored strategies to capitalize on these insights. These strategies might include launching new products, optimizing existing processes or adopting cutting-edge technologies. To foster a culture of creativity within the organization, consultants often lead brainstorming sessions, workshops, and design thinking exercises, encouraging team members to think outside the box and generate novel ideas. Their role extends to managing the implementation of these innovative projects, ensuring they are executed efficiently and within budget. This involves coordinating efforts across different departments, managing timelines, and addressing any challenges that arise to keep the projects on track.

Innovation consultants aren't only about managing projects. At its most basic level, essentially their job means making sure the great ideas they create are actually working well. They look at everything for instance, if a company is making more money because of them, if it's running more smoothly and if customers are happier but it's not primarily focused on the numbers and plans. These consultants also meet with the top heads of the company to help them create a tenor in the company that keeps everyone coming up with bright ideas. They may potentially suggest making small changes, like changing who does what or spending money in different ways to keep the ideas flowing and the company quick on its feet: asking for ideas from people outside the company is another large thing they do. They connect with new businesses and intelligent and informed at universities to pull in new thinking and tools, making sure the businesses they help don't fall behind because everything changes very quickly. Being an innovation consultant is perfect for someone who's first rate at a significant number of things but an expert at one, since you're always entering into different projects but really get to delve deep into what you're best at. This mix of skills and knowing different items is extremely useful when figuring out how to tackle new challenges it helps to stand out and come up with solutions that others might not think of.

Innovation consulting requires a broad skill set that spans various domains, along with deep expertise in at least one area. This combination allows consultants to effectively understand and integrate multiple perspectives while providing specialized knowledge that can drive significant value. One good thing about such a role is that since you work on multiple industries and new things almost every time the chance of repeated and monotonous activities is very less, so basically you have an exciting job every day!

Firstly, the broad knowledge base of a "jack of all trades" is crucial in innovation consulting because it involves working across different industries and functions. Consultants need to understand market trends, customer behaviours, technological advancements, and operational processes. Having a wide range of skills enables them to draw connections between seemingly unrelated fields, leading to unique and innovative solutions. This versatility allows innovation consultants to adapt to various challenges and leverage different methodologies and tools, making them highly effective in identifying and capitalizing on new opportunities.

Secondly, being a "master of one" complements the broad skill set by providing a depth of expertise that can be crucial for specific aspects of a project. Whether it's in technology, marketing, product development, or any other specialized field, having deep knowledge allows consultants to offer authoritative insights and drive key aspects of the innovation process. This mastery ensures that while they can see the big picture, they also bring substantial value to critical components of the project, ensuring high-quality outcomes and informed decision-making.

In essence, the innovation consultant role benefits greatly from individuals who can blend a wide-ranging understanding of multiple domains with deep expertise in one area. This combination enhances their ability to deliver comprehensive and impactful solutions, making them invaluable assets to any organization looking to innovate and stay competitive.

Currently there are tools like Sonara and LoopCV two which I have tried personally so I can write about them, there could be more and better ones too but the reason I give example as usual is with the understanding that my audience is smart enough to find out what is relevant at the time the user is reading the book, let us take Sonara job application portal.

I think such AI tool has the potential to change the industry for job hunting, called Sonara. It's all about making the search for Innovation Consultant jobs a whole lot easier. It makes every single step of finding a job smoother, all the way from finding job listings to getting those prized interviews lined up. Sonara gets to know all about your job needs and work history from you, then uses that data to hunt down new opportunities on the Internet without missing a beat. When Sonara spots a good match for someone looking to be an Innovation Consultant, it doesn't only put your name in the list. It digs into what the job needs and compares that to what you're good at, and the things you've done before, this way it quickly marks you as a really strong fit even before you've hit apply. And since it sends out your applications for you, completely dialled into what employers want to see in terms of keywords and all, it's not simply about throwing your resume at as many places as hoping for the best.

By doing things this way, it's not only about making applying quicker, it actually amps up your chance of getting noticed by big companies on the lookout for someone who thinks differently. And we may thus possibly come up with a direct conclusion that all AI machine's learning isn't only special technology talk, it could genuinely help you get in front of the right eyeballs in the innovation consulting arena.

Moreover, Sonara's continuous learning capabilities mean it adapts its search criteria based on feedback and emerging trends in the job market. This ensures that my job search remains dynamic and responsive to evolving demands within the innovation consultancy field. By entrusting Sonara to handle the repetitive tasks of job hunting, you can redirect your energy towards honing your consulting skills, fostering industry connections, and staying abreast of cutting-edge developments.

For this section, let us engage in a talk about how in the concentrated environment, or world of extremely-fast changing technology, firms searching for the next big technology really create an impact. These places don't only keep doing what they are used to instead, they're always watching for new ideas from other areas. By doing this, they're not simply trying new and different options and keeping the feeling of creativity alive they're also getting ready to start new big trends before everyone else notices. They think ahead, aiming to be leaders in bringing in new material.

Yet another great opportunity is tech scouting, you can be the bridge that connects the technology with right technology that solves the problem, it is like a referral for technology that solves a problem for the client. This could pay off thousands of dollars just be technology leads. Technology Scouting is the process of discovering, analysing, and evaluating new or existing technologies that will help them with their innovation process. In simple terms, it is a process for companies to find the necessary technology outside the company. It is an important aspect of the open innovation strategy. This serves as a powerful catalyst for innovation by bringing diverse perspectives and fresh insights into the organization.

The upshot of this entire piece is, clearly, that looking for wonderful technology outside your own company can be extremely helpful. There's technology scouting and it means companies are on the lookout for other businesses or intelligent and informed people outside their own walls who are doing amazing things with technology. Instead of just sticking to what they know inside their own company they reach out and find experts or fresh technology in the area; this is of significant consequence because it means they're not missing out on amazing inventions or ideas just because it wasn't made at their location. By partnering up with these outside professionals or young companies just filled with new ideas, businesses can really hone their approach, they could make their products significantly better, get things done more efficiently or even come up with something completely new that amazes everyone.

Moreover, tech scouting serves as a strategic initiative to mitigate risks associated with relying solely on internal R&D efforts. By diversifying their technological inputs and staying abreast of developments in adjacent industries or emerging sectors, organizations can better anticipate future trends and disruptions. This foresight not only bolsters their resilience but also positions them as proactive players in shaping industry standards and driving industry-wide innovation. Beyond its strategic benefits, tech scouting fosters a culture of openness and collaboration within organizations. By actively engaging with external innovators and thought leaders, companies cultivate a dynamic ecosystem where ideas flow freely and partnerships flourish. This collaborative spirit not only enriches internal processes but also nurtures a mindset of continuous learning and adaptation, essential for thriving in an increasingly competitive and rapidly evolving technological landscape.

In essence, tech scouting represents a forward-thinking approach to innovation one that recognizes the value of external expertise and embraces the potential of collaborative partnerships. By actively seeking out and engaging with external companies leads, organizations position themselves at the forefront of technological advancement, ready to harness new opportunities and drive sustainable growth in a dynamic global economy.

When you place yourself into innovation competitions and new activities, you're really opening up some spectacular doors. Besides getting to demonstrate your skills, you get to convene with specialists, maybe meet your next leader, or meet and talk to people who could want what you're selling down the line. If you end up winning or even just making it to the final round, that's a clear signal to everyone that you're really good at what you do. It's basically proof that you are smart and good at coming up with new ideas, which leaders and clients like. In addition, all the content you create and figure out while you're at these events strengthens drastically your portfolio, making it a strong presentation of all your knowledge and how you solve difficult problems. A discerning reader may begin to register that diving deep into these challenge puzzles not only makes you sharper but also starts setting you up as a major player, the kind others look up to for intelligent and informed moves in the whole innovation advisory scene. Staying active and scoring wins in these arenas slowly but surely carves out your name as someone who's really going places, especially in the concentrated environment, or world of innovation consultancy, shaping a path for a future that's nothing short of amazing.

Givemechallenge.com features opportunities from all over the world, making it a valuable resource for international participants looking for opportunities in global competitions and gain recognition. Users can subscribe to receive notifications and updates about new challenges and deadlines, ensuring they don't miss out on opportunities. Users gain access to a wide range of opportunities that they might not find through other means.

Participating in these challenges helps individuals develop and showcase their skills, from problem-solving and creativity to technical expertise. We are also on the way of developing a certificate verification process where in we plan to centrally certify various innovation challenges you have won which users can showcase to potential employers.

So in a nut shell by strengthening and ensuring regular updates at Givemechallenge.com along with the release of this book, users and especially the readers of my book will never run out of innovation opportunities, there won't be any need for you to look for various innovation opportunities elsewhere because we plan to make Givemechallenge the master or the parent of aggregating all the opportunities, you can support us by helping sharing a word about the portal and various innovation opportunities. You can also visit Givemechallenge.com by scanning the QR code found in the steam coming out of the cup in the cover page of this book, let that be the take away from this book.

CHAPTER IV

How to Increase Your Chances of Winning a Challenge

"If you want to shine like a sun, first burn like a sun - Dr. A.P.J. Abdul Kalam"

Based on my experience of winning 60+ global innovation challenges at the time of writing this book, I can summarize some of the best practices, you can use this to draw inspiration, there is no fixed formula for success, you will have to always observe and improvise based on the opportunity though.

1. Take time to Understand the Challenge, there is a reason the client is looking for solution from public, organizations like NASA already have some of the best brain not only in the town but in the entire world, as these organizations are talent magnets to attract the best brain, so you need to understand the seriousness of the problem the client is facing, if you try to solve the problem only with a perspective of an existing employee of NASA or scientist for example you may not win the challenge, what they are often looking for a is a totally new perspective that nobody in the organization has ever thought through, the out of the box thinking solutions as you might have heard off.

2. Conduct comprehensive research on the problem or opportunity addressed by the challenge. Explore existing solutions, market trends, customer needs, and technological advancements relevant to the challenge.

3. Take the time to thoroughly understand the goals, criteria, and constraints of the innovation challenge. Clarify any ambiguities and ensure that you have a clear understanding of what is

expected, don't hesitate to contact the challenge organizers to contact directly to make sure you are submitting a proposal that is geared towards the solution they are looking for.

4. The client is throwing away rewards and cash to get a solution, this means if it was something that they can research out from books and web, they wouldn't have the need for conducting a crowdsourcing innovation challenge at the first place, their internal team itself could only have done this.

If you ask me for the single most important way to increase your chances of winning a challenge, it's staying updated on the latest tech news and market technologies, if you are aware of some latest technologies then you can use that to apply for some of the innovation challenges to solve problems, especially new innovative digital tools can help you save time, innovate better and increase your productivity. You should be continuously hunting for various innovative products and technology that will help you apply the new ideas and pack it as a solution for various innovation challenges. One such platform I use is for last few years for digital products is "Producthunt" . If you read through latest tech news that also helps, I came across a glue that will turn extremely sticky when a particular wavelength of light is passed through it and unsticks when another wavelength of light is applied, this technology was successfully applied by me in multiple innovation challenges, one of it was as ancillary lights for automobiles where I could successfully apply this tech and solve their problem. Another example I can quote where reading technology news and keeping myself has helped me crack innovation challenge was a large pharmaceutical company was looking for improving the experience of giving medicine for the kids, around that time I came across about this technology news about digital lollipop that is when a small tiny amount of current is applied to taste buds it can simulate various taste without any harm, I went ahead and proposed to integrate the same within a spoon which can be used to give cough syrup and other oral medicine to kids, the spoon will be placed on the tongue of the kids and using digital lollipop technology it will simulate a sweet taste which is good enough to mask the sour or bitter taste of the medicine and hence improving the medicine experience for the kids, this went on to win an award for me again, the point I am trying to make here is the importance of staying updated about the various technologies in the market which enabled me to propose such solutions.

Increasing your chances of winning a challenge begins with a deep understanding of the evaluation criteria. Each innovation challenge has specific metrics and standards that judges use to assess submissions. These criteria often include aspects such as originality, feasibility, impact, and presentation. Good thing is that most of the innovation challenges nowadays provide you with this information based on my experience. By carefully studying these guidelines, you can tailor your approach to meet and exceed the expectations. Start by thoroughly reading the challenge brief and any additional documentation provided. Pay close attention to the weight given to each criterion, as this will help you prioritize your efforts accordingly.

One effective strategy is to align your solution directly with the evaluation criteria. For instance, if originality is highly valued, focus on highlighting what makes your idea unique and how it differs from existing solutions. If feasibility is a key criterion, provide detailed evidence of how your solution can be realistically implemented, including prototypes, pilot tests, or data-driven projections. By clearly demonstrating how your submission meets each specific criterion, you make it easier for judges to recognize the strengths of your proposal. Understanding the evaluation criteria also means anticipating potential questions or concerns that judges might have. Put yourself in their shoes and critically assess your submission. Are there any areas that might raise doubts about feasibility or impact? Address these proactively within your proposal. For example, if scalability is important, outline a clear plan for how your solution can be expanded and adapted over time. If your solution is applicable to a particular geography then craft your solution with this in mind. By pre-emptively addressing possible weaknesses, you can strengthen your submission and build confidence in your idea.

Lastly, effective communication plays a crucial role in aligning your submission with the evaluation criteria. Ensure that your proposal is well-organized and clearly articulates how it meets each criterion. Use visuals, diagrams, and concise explanations to make complex ideas more accessible. A compelling narrative that ties together the problem, solution, and its potential impact can help engage judges and make your submission memorable. Remember, judges are not just looking for good ideas, they are looking for ideas that are well-presented and easy to understand. By mastering the art of clear communication and aligning with the evaluation criteria, you significantly enhance your chances of winning the challenge.

There are many innovation challenges that happens yearly, like various design awards, one segment many people don't focus is previous winners, you spend some time to discover their winning submission and their winning journey and what they do and what they did to win. Learning from past winners is one of the most effective ways to increase your chances of winning a challenge. Past winners often have valuable insights and strategies that can provide a roadmap for success. One key tip from previous winners is to thoroughly understand the problem statement and go beyond the surface level. Dive deep into the issue you're addressing and ensure your solution is comprehensive and well-researched. This depth of understanding allows you to craft a solution that not only meets the challenge requirements but also anticipates potential issues and provides robust, thoughtful answers.

I found it even more beneficial to learn from runner ups and ideas that didn't make it to the first prize where you are presented with an opportunity to learn the reason for their failure at the expense of their failure, which will also help you avoid the same.

"Don't read success stories, you will only get a message.
Read failure stories, you will get some ideas to get success -
Dr. A.P.J. Abdul Kalam"

Another tip from past winners is the importance of storytelling in your submission. Winning entries often tell a compelling story that clearly communicates the problem, the proposed solution, and the anticipated impact. By framing your idea within a narrative, you can engage the judges emotionally and intellectually. This approach makes your submission more memorable and helps convey the significance and potential of your idea in a relatable way. Use real-world examples, user testimonials, and compelling visuals to bring your story to life and make a strong impression.

Collaboration and leveraging diverse skills within your team is another common theme among past winners. Winning teams often consist of individuals with different backgrounds and expertise, allowing them to tackle the problem from multiple angles. This interdisciplinary approach can lead to more innovative and well-rounded solutions. Past winners suggest forming a team that includes technical experts, designers, and business strategists to cover all bases. Effective teamwork and clear communication within the team can also enhance the quality of your submission by ensuring that all aspects of the challenge are addressed thoroughly.

Finally, attention to detail and adherence to guidelines cannot be overstated. Past winners emphasize the importance of meticulously following the challenge instructions and submission guidelines. This includes meeting all the formatting requirements, respecting word limits, and submitting all necessary documents on time. Even the most innovative idea can be overlooked if it fails to comply with the basic requirements. Past winners recommend double-checking your submission for any errors or omissions and possibly seeking feedback from mentors or peers before finalizing it. By ensuring that every detail is polished and professional, you demonstrate your commitment and increase your credibility in the eyes of the judges.

CHAPTER V

Characteristics of Winning Ideas

A man sitting lost in his own thoughts

As mentioned earlier I used to post close to 40+ Innovation challenges in Givemechallenge.com during a time myself on a daily basis, often once the challenge is over the challenge sponsors used to contact me to publish the winners also, this gave me an opportunity to check out the winning contributions of 1000's of challenges and I used to take time to research and study the winning solutions and draw patterns from them to identify the winning recipe that I was looking for, at that time I was looking for this recipe so that I can use this winning recipe to flavour my own submissions so that it wins, little did I knew at that time I would be writing a book about it to tell and share my experience with a larger audience. Here are few observations of mine including my experience in participating over 1000+ innovation challenges. Yes, that is right, I have participated in over 1000+ innovation challenge this is not something that I did over a week, month or a year, it is spanned over 15+ years. Let me introduce you to some math here. Let us assume it is 15 years, that is approximately 5475 days, that is around 1 competition participation in 5.5 days, the key is consistency. My winning rate is around 6% as you would have guessed, so indeed this a tough job, if it was easy everyone would do this right?

Also what you need to understand is that you are solving problems that the some of the best minds in the relevant industry is not able to solve, the sense of satisfaction that this brought to me was immense and this motivated me and fuelled me to submit even multiple submissions for a single challenge. One of the most intriguing aspects of my journey with innovation challenges has been my close interaction with both the challenges themselves and their outcomes. My initial intent was to identify patterns to enhance my own submissions, but over time, this analysis evolved into a deeper passion for understanding the core attributes of successful innovations.

During this extensive process, I noticed several recurring characteristics in the winning ideas. Firstly, originality was a hallmark of success. Originality is a crucial factor. Judges and organizers are often looking for fresh perspectives and novel approaches that break away from conventional solutions. An idea that introduces a new concept or a unique way of addressing a problem tends to stand out. Originality doesn't always mean inventing something entirely new; it can also involve a creative reimagining of existing solutions to make them more effective or accessible.

Winning submissions often presented solutions that were not only innovative but also uniquely tailored to the specific problem at hand. These ideas were fresh and avoided clichés, demonstrating a clear departure from conventional thinking. This originality was often coupled with a strong practical component, where the solutions were not just theoretical but demonstrated a clear path to implementation.

Another key trait of winning ideas was their scalability. Successful innovations were designed with the future in mind, addressing immediate needs while also having the potential to be expanded or adapted for broader application. This forward-thinking approach made the solutions not only relevant but also sustainable in the long run. It was evident that the judges valued ideas that could grow and evolve, providing long-term benefits beyond the initial challenge. This practical approach reassures judges that the idea can move beyond the conceptual stage and be brought to life, addressing the challenge effectively within the given constraints.

Scalability ensures that the idea can grow and evolve, providing long-term value beyond the immediate challenge. This forward-thinking approach is highly valued as it shows that the innovator has considered the broader impact and future applications of their solution, making it a more attractive and sustainable option.

Feasibility played a crucial role in determining the success of a submission. Winning ideas were backed by solid research and data, showcasing their practicality. This meant that the solutions were not just innovative but also realistically achievable within the given constraints. Detailed plans, prototypes, and even small-scale tests were often part of these submissions, proving that the ideas could be effectively brought to life.

Another observation was the importance of clear and compelling communication. The best ideas were those that were articulated well, with a clear problem statement, proposed solution, and expected impact. Submissions that could tell a compelling story and engage the judges on an emotional and intellectual level tended to perform better. This underscored the importance of not only having a great idea but also being able to present it effectively.

Interdisciplinary collaboration was another common feature among winning submissions. Solutions that drew from diverse fields of knowledge and integrated various perspectives were more likely to succeed. This approach not only enriched the quality of the ideas but also demonstrated a broader understanding of the problem, making the solutions more robust and comprehensive.

In terms of my personal experience, participating in over 1,000 innovation challenges over 15 years has taught me the value of persistence and consistency. With approximately one competition every 5.5 days, maintaining a steady pace of participation was crucial. My win rate of around 6% highlights the competitive nature of these challenges, where even the best minds face tough competition. The key takeaway here is that persistence pays off, and each submission, win or lose, is a learning opportunity.

What also became clear is that innovation challenges are about solving real-world problems that even industry experts struggle with. This realization brought immense satisfaction and fuelled my motivation to keep pushing the boundaries. The sense of accomplishment derived from contributing meaningful solutions to complex problems is incomparable and serves as a powerful motivator to continue participating. Through this extensive journey, I've learned that the recipe for a winning idea is a blend of originality, scalability, feasibility, effective communication, and interdisciplinary collaboration. These elements, combined with persistence and a passion for problem-solving, can significantly increase the chances of success in innovation challenges.

One of the most defining characteristics of winning ideas in innovation challenges is their strong user-centric focus. Successful solutions often start with a deep understanding of the target users and their needs. This involves engaging with potential users, gathering their feedback, and ensuring the solution addresses their pain points effectively. By centring the design and functionality around user needs, innovators create products and services that resonate more deeply and are more likely to be adopted.

A compelling value proposition is another crucial element. Winning ideas clearly articulate the unique benefits they offer and how they differentiate from existing solutions. This involves not only identifying the problem but also convincingly demonstrating how the proposed solution is superior. A strong value proposition helps judges and stakeholders quickly grasp the potential impact and advantages of the idea, making it more persuasive and appealing.

Simplicity and elegance in design often distinguish top-tier submissions. Winning ideas typically embody the principle of simplicity, making complex problems easier to solve with straightforward, intuitive solutions. An elegant design is not only aesthetically pleasing but also enhances functionality and user experience. This balance between form and function ensures that the solution is both effective and user-friendly.

In winning ideas you will also see commitment of the time and effort of the person who is proposing the solution, they will go above and beyond to make the solution happen, one of the recent innovation challenge I noticed a team went ahead and applied for a provisional patent for a small design change in a product, this earned them the top prize, the other solutions didn't have a patent or didn't apply for patent, patent application is expensive, so this shows the level of commitment too and it shows that the team was serious in taking the solution forward.

Impact assessment is another key trait of successful ideas. Innovators who can quantify the potential impact of their solution, whether it's in terms of cost savings, efficiency gains, environmental benefits, or social improvements have a significant advantage. Providing metrics or projections that illustrate the real-world effects of the solution helps judges understand its significance and potential for making a difference.

Integration with existing systems and processes also plays a critical role in the success of an idea. Winning solutions often seamlessly fit into current infrastructures, making them easier to implement and more likely to be adopted. This requires a thorough understanding of the existing ecosystem and designing the solution to complement or enhance it without causing significant disruption. There was one innovation challenge that I won were it was asked to come up with innovation to prevent the spreading of carbon powder during loading, cutting and drying processes, here in this case the working of existing system was crucial and how economical it would be retrofit the proposed solution.

Sustainability and ethical considerations are increasingly important in judging innovation challenges. Ideas that take into account environmental impact, resource efficiency, and ethical implications tend to stand out. This demonstrates that the innovators are not only focused on solving a problem but are also committed to doing so in a responsible and sustainable manner.

In one of the innovation challenges, the core challenge was on plastic recycling, as advised by our mentor we emphasized on other ethical factors like waste sorting manually by workers by staring a conveyor full of waste entire day which is very mundane job and with our proposed sorting solution it will make a positive impact in the lives of people sorting waste.

Another characteristic of winning ideas is the presence of a clear roadmap for implementation. This includes detailed steps, timelines, and resource requirements needed to bring the idea to fruition. A well-thought-out plan reassures judges that the team has thoroughly considered the practicalities of deployment and is prepared to take the necessary steps to realize their vision.

Flexibility and adaptability are also vital. Successful innovations are those that can evolve based on feedback and changing circumstances. This involves being open to iteration and improvements, which is crucial for refining the solution and ensuring it remains relevant and effective over time. Flexibility in design and approach allows the solution to be more resilient in the face of unforeseen challenges.

Effective team collaboration and dynamics are often behind winning ideas. Teams that work well together, leveraging each member's strengths and fostering an environment of mutual respect and creativity, tend to produce more innovative and robust solutions. A cohesive team can efficiently tackle complex problems, navigate challenges, and refine their ideas through collaborative effort.

Having a mentor for your team or project who has good expertise in the field you are solving the problem will also help in come up with a solid & robust solution for the problem as an experienced mentor will know all the challenges and issues from an industry perspective and can raise all the questions that jury would have, if you can address and have answers for all of them then it gives you an added advantage over the competitors.

Winning ideas are also driven by passionate people so passion and commitment to the problem being solved can significantly influence the success of an idea. Winning teams are often those who are genuinely passionate about their project, driven by a desire to make a meaningful impact. This passion translates into a higher level of dedication, resilience, and enthusiasm, which can be contagious and compelling to judges and stakeholders. Passionate teams are more likely to persist through challenges and stay committed to their vision, increasing the likelihood of their idea's success.

As I share my experiences and insights in this book, my aim is to provide a roadmap for aspiring innovators. By understanding and applying these characteristics, you can enhance your own submissions and contribute to solving some of the world's most pressing challenges. Whether you're new to innovation challenges or a seasoned participant, I hope this guide will inspire you to think creatively and approach problems with a fresh perspective.

The journey of participating in and analysing thousands of innovation challenges has been both challenging and rewarding. The patterns and insights I've gathered not only helped me improve my own submissions but also inspired me to share these learnings with a broader audience. By embracing these characteristics of winning ideas, you too can embark on a path of innovation and make a significant impact.

CHAPTER VI

How to Put Your Ideas to Practice & Can Ideas Be Recycled?

A boy searching for ideas in a book

My first assignment was for Innocentive when I was in my 10th standard now the platform is known as Wazoku, where I have provided U.S.A department of energy on providing heating solution for the houses using zeolites, I came to know about zeolites from CBSE science text book to be honest.

Later when I reached college we had to give a final year seminar as part of our curriculum, I prepared many topics and finalized a topic on additive manufacturing and 3D printing, we had to write the chosen topic in the college registrar, I went and wrote my topic with date and signed it, then I started preparing the complete seminar, to my surprise few hours before the seminar in the register I could see my topic was struck of with pen and another colleague has chosen my same topic for the seminar. I was left with no time to prepare for my seminar and it carried a good 50 marks. The reason I bring up this instance is to highlight the importance of reusability or recycling of your ideas, I went ahead and presented a seminar on how zeolites can be used for heating of houses, since I have studied and researched the topic in detail and I am the innovator of the idea there is nothing much anyone could copy and present, I also had full knowledge about the topic, to my surprise I got 50/50 in the seminar as the solution was novel and unlike usual topics presented in the seminar. One good thing about mechanical engineering is that we could fit any engineering topic into it.

To effectively put your ideas into practice, you need a clear roadmap that begins with identifying and understanding the problem you're solving. This involves extensive research to ensure that your idea is viable and can address the issue at hand. In my case mentioned above, discovering zeolites in my CBSE science textbook sparked an idea. Your subsequent research on their properties and potential applications, like in heating solutions, exemplifies the importance of understanding the problem deeply before proposing a solution.

After thorough research, the next step is planning and prototyping. A well-thought-out plan outlines the steps needed to bring your idea to life. Prototyping, whether through physical models or simulations, allows you to test the feasibility of your concept. When I proposed the zeolite-based heating solution, creating a prototype could have helped in visualizing its practical applications and identifying potential challenges early on.

Collaboration is crucial in the implementation phase. Sharing my ideas with others, such as through platforms like Wazoku, brings diverse perspectives and expertise that can enhance your concept. Collaboration can provide valuable feedback and open up new possibilities that you might not have considered. When I submitted My idea to the U.S. Department of Energy, the collaborative nature of such platforms allowed My idea to gain traction and be evaluated by experts.

Adapting and refining your idea based on feedback is another essential step. No idea is perfect from the outset, and being open to constructive criticism helps in refining it. The feedback that I have received from presenting my zeolite heating solution likely helped me improve and solidify my concept today and I still can reuse the same technology to solves other problems too. Iterative refinement ensures that the final implementation is robust and effective.

Understanding the market and user needs is also critical. Even the best ideas can fail if they don't meet the needs or preferences of the target audience. Conducting market research to gauge the potential acceptance of your solution ensures that your idea is not only innovative but also practical and desired. My zeolite heating solution, for instance, would need to be evaluated for its cost-effectiveness and ease of use in typical household settings.

Securing resources is a vital aspect of bringing ideas to practice. This includes funding, materials, and human resources. Identifying potential sources of funding, such as grants, investors, or partnerships, is essential. In my case, presenting to a government department likely provided access to the resources needed for further development of your idea.

Recycling ideas involves reusing and adapting them for different contexts or problems. My experience with the zeolite heating solution demonstrates this well. When my original seminar topic was taken, I have successfully recycled my previous idea to my advantage, showcasing its adaptability and the deep understanding of the subject. This adaptability not only saved me in a tight situation but also highlighted the versatility of the innovation.

Finally, documenting your journey and learning from the process is essential. Keeping a record of your research, planning and implementation phases, the ideas that you have submitted to various challenges is a treasure house or firework of stimuli when you further dig out any solutions for any other innovation challenges or competitions, you will be surprised to see how easily you can connect your old ideas and use as inspirations to new ideas since these are your original ideas, if you have single image representations of your ideas just glancing at your old ideas and submissions could also work great, this is not happening based on chance and there is of course science behind this which is important and I would like to explain a bit more here as I believe this can help.

How It Is Easy to Build Upon Your Own Ideas: A Neuronal and Scientific Perspective?

Neuroplasticity visualized

From a scientific and neuronal standpoint, building upon your own ideas is often easier due to the brain's inherent mechanisms and cognitive processes. Here's a detailed explanation.

The human brain is composed of a vast network of neurons that communicate through synapses. When I first encounter a concept, such as zeolites in my CBSE science textbook, specific neural pathways are activated and strengthened through repetition and reinforcement. This process is known as synaptic plasticity. As you continue to research and think about zeolites, these neural connections become stronger and more efficient, embedding the knowledge into my long-term memory.

The hippocampus, a critical brain region for memory formation, works in conjunction with the cerebral cortex, where long-term memories are stored. Initially, my detailed study of zeolites heavily involves the hippocampus. Over time, this information is gradually transferred to the cortex for long-term storage. This transfer allows me to recall and build upon this information with greater ease, as the neural pathways are well-established.

Neuroplasticity is the brain's ability to reorganize itself by forming new neural connections throughout life. When I revisit my previous idea about zeolites for a seminar, the brain's plasticity allows me to refine and expand upon this idea more efficiently. My brain can connect existing knowledge with new information, enhancing creativity and innovation.

According to Knowledge Frameworks Schema Theory, the brain organizes knowledge into schemas or mental frameworks. When you initially learn about a topic, you create a basic schema. As you acquire more information, you expand and modify this schema. Yes similar to the schemas that we have in SQL!

In the case of your zeolite heating solution, my initial schema from the CBSE textbook was expanded through further research and application, making it easier to build upon. Chunking is a cognitive process where the brain groups information into manageable units or chunks. By thoroughly understanding zeolites and their properties, I have created chunks of related information. When we need to develop or present new ideas, these chunks make it easier to retrieve and apply the information efficiently.

Metacognition or thinking about thinking, allows you to be aware of your cognitive processes. My deep understanding of the zeolite topic likely involved metacognitive strategies, such as self-questioning and reflection, which facilitated a deeper comprehension. This awareness helps in identifying gaps in my knowledge and focusing on areas that need further development, making it easier to build on my ideas.

Various Engaging activities with your idea through research, prototyping, and collaboration reinforces neural connections. This active learning process helps solidify your understanding and makes it easier to recall and expand upon your ideas. When I presented my zeolite heating solution, the preparation and presentation further reinforced my knowledge, making subsequent enhancements more straightforward.

Applying your idea to solve real-world problems engages critical thinking and problem-solving skills. This application helps in refining and improving the idea.

Receiving feedback and adapting your idea accordingly is crucial for improvement. Feedback mechanisms engage the brain's reward system, reinforcing positive changes and encouraging further refinement. The feedback I received during my seminar presentation not only validated your knowledge but also provided insights for further enhancements.

Building upon your own ideas is facilitated by the brain's complex neuronal structures and cognitive processes. The strengthening of neural connections through repeated exposure and active engagement, combined with cognitive strategies like schema development, chunking, and metacognition, makes it easier to refine and expand upon existing ideas. This scientific understanding underscores why revisiting and enhancing your concepts, such as me revisiting innovative use of zeolites, is both effective and efficient.

I hope this reflection on my experience with both the zeolite heating solution and the seminar incident provides valuable lessons in resilience, adaptability the importance of thorough preparation and importance of reuse of your ideas which can help you think ideas quickly, participate and provide innovative solutions better.

CHAPTER VII

How to Sell & Monetize Your Ideas

If you're thinking about making money from your ideas, it's not simply about having a intelligent and informed thought. You must be able to put your idea into words that explain why it's worth something in a strong and easy-to-understand way. It's not simple, you must get people's attention by showing exactly how your idea is the answer they've been looking for or the door to something they've wanted. Next, we engage in an intense examination of locking down your idea with items such as patents, copyrights, or making people sign agreements that they won't steal your innovation. This ensures you are recognized for your creativity and get paid for it. Chase down the right people who might want to hear what you must say, it could be big companies, could be individual leaders, or just about anyone with the money to invest actually, turning your idea into a lot of money revolves less around the idea itself and more around how you sell it. In essence, you've really got to highlight why your invention is fantastic and protect it, then find the right audience to sell it.

To really sell an idea and make some money out of it, you must comprehend how it fits into the market and be smooth about demonstrating why it's going to work. It's not only about having a marvellous idea, you need to actually convince people, mixing in a bit of creativity, being good at speaking to others and knowing a bit about business. When you're trying to win someone over, you must reconfigure your approach based on who you're speaking to, showing them exactly why your idea is something they need. In addition, there can possibly be gratification in your knowing that not sticking rigidly to your first idea but adjusting it as you go based on what others say can make it even more appealing. And sometimes you must team up with others who've got what you need to get your idea off the ground. In the end, raking in cash from your idea is possible but get ready it's going to take patience, a plan of action, and knowing how to successfully deal with the fraught parts of owning your wisdom and working with others.

Other approach is to think out ideas by looking at the needs or problems of the others that is where innovation challenges come into picture, there are thousands of innovation challenges or competitions around the world where companies and organizations are looking for ideas and solutions to their problems, so if you can think out relevant ideas that can solve their problems then you can provide them your ideas in exchange of rewards and monetary benefits.

If you have product idea then if you want to sell it, it becomes important to patent it and you will find it easier to sell it when you have a patent, now it is much easier to patent your ideas with the help of artificial intelligence, what used to cost thousands of dollars for drafting a patent submission has become a DIY task with certain tool, since I think this will add value to my readers and is important I would give a high level overview on how to do this and I am sure my readers are smart enough to pick up from what I explain here and figure out the rest.

Here's a detailed breakdown of the patent drafting process using LM Studio with the Vicuna 13B model. The reason we are not using ChatGPT is due to the confidentiality reason, by using LM studio you can run large language models locally in your system ensuring confidentiality.

As the First you will have to download and install LM Studio, a graphical user interface for running large language models (LLMs) locally. Download the Vicuna 13B model from Hugging Face and load it into LM Studio. You can try out various other LLM models too.

We will use LM Studio to prepare the necessary information for the patent application, including:

• Title of the Invention: A concise title describing the invention.

- Current State-of-the-Art: Bullet points highlighting the current state of technology.
- Disadvantages of the State-of-the-Art: Points describing the limitations or issues with the current technology.
- Objective of the Invention: A clear statement of what the invention aims to achieve.
- Set of Claims: Detailed claims defining the scope and specifics of the invention.

Use specific prompts to guide the LLM in drafting different sections of the patent application. For this, users can use a personal prompting template library. User can provide a prompt like "You are a patent attorney. I want you to write a European patent application with me. First, let's write the section technical field."

Input: Include the title of the invention.

Example Output: "The present invention generally relates to the field of artificial intelligence (AI) and computer-assisted patent prosecution, and more particularly to techniques for utilizing AI algorithms and natural language processing (NLP) to assist patent attorneys and examiners in the drafting, review, and prosecution of patent applications."

Drafting the Background Section:

Prompt: Use a prompt for the background section, including context information such as the current state of the art, disadvantages, and objectives.

Input:Patent drafting is a highly manual task. Some patent attorneys perceive patent drafting more as an art form than an engineering activity. Writing the claims requires human intellect and strategic decisions, but once the claims are finalized, writing up the rest of the patent application involves a large portion of easy, repetitive tasks. AI and LLMs are currently not used in production due to confidentiality concerns. The objective is to enable a more streamlined patent drafting process through AI automation in a secure manner.

Example Output: The AI processes the input and generates a detailed background section.

Drafting the Summary Section of Claim One:

Prompt: Provide a prompt for drafting the summary section of claim one.

Input: Claim one: "A software product comprising one or more function modules each configured to assist a user in one or more tasks for drafting a patent application, wherein at least one of the function modules is configured to access an AI system comprising one or more language models, wherein the AI system executes within a secured computing environment."

Technical advantage: "The secured computing environment enables secure use of AI for patent drafting without jeopardizing the novelty of the invention or the confidentiality requirements of the drafter."

Example Output: The AI breaks down the claim into individual elements and provides explanations and advantages for each element.

Drafting Dependent Claims:

Prompt: Use a prompt for drafting dependent claims with style and formatting instructions.

Input: Provide the dependent claims and necessary context.

Example Output: The AI generates a set of dependent claims formatted and styled according to the input instructions.

For compilation and review, copy the outputs from the LLM into a prepared document with sections like the technical field, background, summary, and claims. Review and refine the draft to ensure accuracy and completeness.

Finally, spend additional time (estimated at around 5 hours) to finalize and expand the AI-generated draft, ensuring it meets all legal and technical requirements. The final product is a high-quality first draft of a patent application, created efficiently using AI assistance. By following these steps, patent attorneys can leverage AI to streamline the patent drafting process, focusing more on strategic and intellectual tasks while automating repetitive and less intellectually demanding parts and if you are a person who is reading this book and you are innovator or inventor then you can skip the help of attorney and seek help from AI to draft your patent application saving you time and thousands of dollars in patent attorney fees.

• • •

The next step would be creating a good looking presentation to pitch your product or a business idea, you can go the traditional route or if you would like to leverage AI tools, you will have advantage here, I would like to explain it with one tool but this is not a promotion, you can use any tool, I will explain it with Beautiful.ai platform, I have chosen this over others because they are professional and well established, I have come across a few smaller platforms too but not citing it in here because I am not sure if they will be around few years from now when people read this book. Even if this platform doesn't exist few years from now the idea is to give my readers a feel of what they need to do and I am sure my readers are smart enough to find suitable alternatives tools wherever required.

Creating a presentation to sell your ideas using Beautiful.ai involves multiple steps. Here's a detailed guide to help you through the process, the process is quite similar with other platform too, I am explaining it in detail so that you can include what is relevant.

First step is to sign up in whatever platform you would like to build AI presentations in this case it is Beautiful.ai. You can sign up using your email or connect through Google or LinkedIn.

Once you have an account, log in to access the dashboard. Start a New Presentation, Click on "New Presentation" from the dashboard. Browse through the available templates and select one that fits the theme and purpose of your presentation. Beautiful.ai offers various templates designed for different types of presentations, including sales pitches.

To create a presentation using Beautiful.ai, Start with your Title Slide, where you should enter the title of your presentation. If needed, add a subtitle or tagline. Include your name, company name, and date, and upload your company logo for branding.

Next, Outline Your Content on an Agenda Slide. Provide an overview of the topics you'll cover and list the main sections like Introduction, Problem, Solution, and Market Opportunity.

For the Content Slides:

- Introduction: Introduce your company and its mission.
- Problem Statement: Clearly define the problem your product or idea addresses.
- Solution: Describe how your product or idea solves the problem.
- Market Opportunity: Present data on market size, target audience, and growth potential.
- Product Features: Highlight the key features and benefits of your product.
- Business Model: Explain how your business makes money.
- Go-to-Market Strategy: Outline your marketing and sales strategy.
- Competition: Analyse competitors and showcase your unique selling proposition.
- Financial Projections: Include forecasts for revenue, expenses, and profits.
- Team: Showcase key team members and their expertise.
- Call to Action: Clearly state what you want from your audience, such as investment or partnership.
- Q&A: Prepare a slide for audience questions.

Utilize Beautiful.ai's features for designing and adding content, Click "Add Slide" to create new slides and choose from different slide types like text, image, or chart. Beautiful.ai's AI-powered design adjusts the layout automatically for a polished look. Use text boxes for headings and content, upload images or use stock images, and create charts and graphs to visualize data.
Customize your presentation by choosing themes that match your brand and adjusting layouts as needed.

Finally, Review and Finalize your presentation. Use the preview feature to check for clarity and coherence, make necessary edits, and collaborate with team members for feedback. Once satisfied, export your presentation as a PowerPoint file, PDF, or share it via a link. Practice delivering your presentation to ensure you are comfortable with the content and flow, then present it using the exported file or shared link.

Using Beautiful.ai simplifies the process of creating visually appealing and well-structured presentations, allowing you to focus more on the content and delivery of your pitch.

● ● ●

Once you have presentation whether it is your business presentation or your school presentation it is all about your delivery, many of you may not be aware of the small feature hiding within Microsoft ppt where you can rehearse your pitch and ppt will give you real time feedback and you will also get a good idea of the time needed for you to pitch, this will give a tremendous boost of your confidence.

Microsoft Presenter Coach is an invaluable tool integrated into PowerPoint that helps you refine your presentation delivery by providing real-time, AI-powered feedback. To use Presenter Coach, start by opening your PowerPoint presentation and clicking on the "Slideshow" tab. From there, select "Rehearse with Coach." As you begin rehearsing, Presenter Coach will analyse your speech and provide instant feedback. One of its standout features is the "Reading from Slide" detector, which alerts you if you are reading directly from your slides too often. This helps ensure you engage more naturally with your audience, making your presentation more dynamic and less monotonous.

In addition to detecting reading from slides, Presenter Coach also checks for the use of inclusive language, which is crucial for creating a respectful and engaging presentation. The tool will suggest alternative phrases if you use terms that may not be inclusive or might alienate parts of your audience. Other features include pacing analysis, helping you maintain an optimal speaking speed, and filler word detection, which alerts you if you're using too many "ums" or "ahs." After rehearsing, you'll receive a detailed report summarizing your performance, including insights on your pacing, use of filler words, and more. This comprehensive feedback enables you to make targeted improvements, ensuring your final presentation is polished and impactful.

I would also like to draw your attention to another class of AI powered tools that will help you master your final sales pitch and have answers to all the questions at your fingertip.

AI role play is an innovative technique for practicing and presenting your pitch, especially useful for preparing to handle difficult questions in high-stakes situations. By engaging with an AI designed to simulate a range of customer or stakeholder responses, you can hone your communication skills and refine your message. There are various platforms that offer such services for pitches and communication like Virtualspeech, you should do some research on this has there are lot of developments happening on daily basis in this space and it is hard for me to suggests what is best because by the time you read the book it may not be relevant and something better might have already come but the idea remains same.

This process trains you to think of solid answers and boosts your confidence when speaking with others about fraught subjects; the AI is set up to ask hard questions, argue or mention the common concerns you'd encounter when discussing with people for real. It sets you on a path to discovery and discernment, prepping you to successfully deal with whatever doubts or problems your listeners might have.

We can take as a definite certainty that the AI role play helps make your presentation approach a lot stronger and more convincing. You get to fine-tune your pitch because, after pretending to interact with someone, the AI tells you clearly where you slipped up or could strengthen drastically your points. With every attempt, you're getting better, ready to face those tough questions without getting complicated, all while keeping it professional, this all leads to you enhancing your chances of performing well when it actually counts.

Effective presentation skills are crucial in today's workplace, and this practice exercise offers you the opportunity to enhance your skills in various virtual settings, such as a conference room, meeting room, lecture hall, classroom, and TEDx-style theatre. After each session, you'll receive detailed feedback on aspects like your pace, use of filler words, pitch, listenability, and, if using VR, eye contact. You can repeat these sessions as often as needed to refine and perfect your presentation abilities.

CHAPTER VIII

Innovation Metrics and Performance Evaluation: How Do You Measure Innovation?

I am firm believer of the fact that we cannot improve something which we cannot measure it, so it is inevitable for us to come up with a solution to measure innovation.

One of the metrics involves tracking the speed at which new ideas are generated within an organization or by an individual. It's not just about quantity but also about the diversity and novelty of these ideas. How rapidly are teams brainstorming, and how efficiently are they moving from concept to prototype?

Ultimately, innovation should contribute to the bottom line. Tracking the revenue generated from new products or services can be a tangible measure of innovation success. This metric not only reflects the effectiveness of innovation but also its market acceptance.

This is no brainer but still I would put it across, Quantifying the number of patents filed and granted can provide insights into the innovation output of a company. However, it's important to also assess the quality and relevance of these patents, as well as their impact on the market. Innovation challenges solved or won could also be a great way to measure the innovation potential.

Innovation competitions and hackathons are powerful tools for recruiting innovative talent, offering a dynamic platform for individuals to showcase their creativity, problem-solving skills, and collaborative abilities. Here's how these events can serve as effective recruitment strategies.

Events such as innovation competitions and fun activities are a major magnet for people from all walks of life. We are looking at students, professionals, entrepreneurs and even parents - all of them excited to demonstrate what they can do, these events let companies pull in the best from different areas and work fields, people who love to create new things and want to share what they know.

These events provide a unique opportunity to identify potential candidates who possess the qualities and capabilities sought by the organization. By observing participants in action, recruiters can assess their technical skills, problem-solving abilities, teamwork and adaptability, gaining valuable insights into their potential fit within the organization.

When you participate in innovation competitions and other events, you really understand a taste of what working for the company is like, they demonstrate how the company loves coming up with new things, working together and always learning. I consider anything that can affect these competitions and truly cares about getting the right people who see things the same way, these events aren't only fun, they're about connecting with more people, from students to professionals and even big names in the industry. Companies get to spread the word about what they're bringing to the table in the whole innovation game and strengthen drastically their image as a great location to work. It's a intelligent and informed move, without a doubt.

They do more than just put the company's name in the area, they bring out the creative best in everyone who joins. You'd be pushed to come up with fresh wisdom and solutions that tackle some pretty serious phenomena the world's facing. If you can do well in these areas, the company's going to notice. It's essentially like proving you've got what it takes to change things in their field. Starting with these events could be a straight shot into getting spectacular opportunities down the line. If a company makes smart choices, keeps in touch, and invests in the people who stand out, they can form a killer team ready for whatever creative challenges come next. Hosting these things? It's about finding young talents who can feel the undercurrent of what the company's all about.

Innovation competitions and hackathons can serve as the starting point for building talent pipelines, allowing organizations to nurture relationships with high-potential candidates over time. By maintaining ongoing communication and engagement with participants, organizations can cultivate a pool of innovative talent who may be suitable for future roles or projects.

These innovation opportunities like hackathons place people into real situations where they have to solve problems and get creative fast, this shows exactly how good someone is technically, how well they work with others and if they're truly innovative, beyond just what their resume says about where they studied or their past job titles. Traditionally, getting hired is mostly about your diplomas and where you've previously worked but new ideas change things. Everyone competes based on what they actually can do, not the school they went to. This evens out the playing field, especially for those extremely skilled people who might not have several special degrees. Utilizing easy tools in picking new employees also introduces a spark of innovation into the company, making it a location in which coming up with wonderful, new ideas isn't simply welcomed, it's part of the daily routine. When a company hires someone because they did a great job on a test, it's pretty likely that person is going to keep coming up with bright ideas that might in fact possibly rub off on everyone else. By relying on this path to discovery and discernment for hiring, companies don't simply stumble upon uncommonly skilled people, they gather a workforce that's ready to innovate no matter the challenge. In addition, by valuing actual skills and the ability to think differently over just a school or job on a resume, businesses can try new and different options with a crew that sees and solves problems in ways nobody else thought of. This is what keeps a business at the top of its trade, constantly moving with the times.

Measuring innovation with a long-term perspective encompasses more than just immediate gains. It's about ensuring that innovation contributes positively to society and the environment, leaving a lasting legacy of progress and sustainability.

Metrics related to environmental impact, social responsibility, and ethical considerations play a crucial role in providing a holistic view of innovation performance.

Assessing the environmental footprint of innovations is essential in today's world. Metrics could include reductions in carbon emissions, water usage, waste generation, and energy consumption resulting from innovative practices or products. Tracking progress toward environmental sustainability goals can help ensure that innovation aligns with broader environmental objectives.

When thinking about inventions, it's extremely important to consider their effects on society, not only how they help businesses grow, things such as whether companies support different types of people and work with local community activities or help with activities for society's wellbeing should be looked at, this is a way to make sure these inventions bring good changes to people's lives and support important social causes. It's also about keeping ethics in the mix, figuring out if these new ideas might be risky or could hurt someone's privacy and making sure everyone's rights are respected during the whole process of coming up with something new.

Perhaps of note (at least to certain readers), we really have to look at whether these innovations are playing by the rules of being fair and not causing any problems, by thinking scrupulously about both the ethical side and how it actually helps or supports people and communities, we can make sure that these inventions are really making things better off for everyone, not only giving businesses a boost.

Now let us see if we don't know or have not seen a person but you only have a resume to find out an innovative person, how can we find the most innovative person just by looking at it.

Looking at resumes to see if someone is first rate at creating new ideas, there are a few key things to look at. An enormous hint something special is going on with the person's skills is if they've worked on all sorts of different projects and in different roles. It shows they are able to handle new situations and solve problems, no matter where they are or what they are working with. When you spot someone has been everywhere, doing many different jobs or tasks, it's a clue they have the mind that can see new ways to solve problems by mixing up what they know from several areas. Another important thing to look for is whether what they've done actually made a difference. It's not simply about having an imagination, it's about getting those ideas in the area and making everything better because of them. If their resume highlights about projects they put into action, things they've made or chipped in on making, or ways they made something work better and can show how it helped, say through making more money, saving costs, or just doing things better, it proves they're not simply about dreams but about making those dreams into something. One may immerse themselves in the knowledge that it's also really important if someone keeps trying to learn more and improve their skills. If they're adding more schooling, picking up new qualifications, showing up at events to learn new skills, or staying on top of the next big thing, that's a sign of someone who doesn't want to stay in one place. They want to lead and keep being first, holding onto whatever new information or technique they can to keep coming up with new ideas. And if you see they're getting involved in groups, contributing to projects everyone can see or join, or going into competitions to share new ideas, that's someone who's not only excited to develop themselves but likes working with others too, including everyone in the search for something new and enjoyable. Now let us try to come up with a simple formula to measure innovation momentum, momentum is a fundamental concept in physics that quantifies the motion possessed by an object. It is defined as the product of an object's mass and velocity let this be our inspiration for innovation momentum formula.

Innovation Momentum (IM):

$$IM = Velocity \times Adaptability \times Resilience^2$$

In this formula:

- Velocity represents the speed at which innovations are conceived and implemented. It's about how quickly the organization can move from ideation to execution. For example, if a company consistently generates new ideas and brings them to market rapidly, it demonstrates high velocity in innovation.
- Adaptability represents the organization's ability to adapt to changing market conditions and customer needs. It reflects how flexible and responsive the organization is to external factors. For instance, if a tech company adjusts its product roadmap swiftly in response to shifts in consumer preferences or technological advancements, it shows high adaptability in innovation.
- Resilience represents the organization's ability to overcome setbacks and challenges in the innovation process. It's about how well the organization can bounce back from failures or unexpected obstacles. For example, if a startup faces a major setback in product development but manages to pivot effectively and eventually succeed, it demonstrates resilience in innovation.

Now, let's consider an example to illustrate how the "Innovation Momentum" formula works.

Imagine a software development company, TechVision, that is known for its innovative products. TechVision launches a new project to develop a cutting-edge mobile application for tracking fitness and wellness metrics. Here's how we can apply the "Innovation Momentum" formula to this scenario:

- Velocity: TechVision's development team works efficiently, quickly translating concepts into prototypes and iterating rapidly based on user feedback. They release a beta version of the app within three months of starting the project, showcasing high velocity in innovation.

- Adaptability: Midway through the development process, TechVision receives feedback from beta testers indicating a need for additional features related to mental health tracking. The team promptly adjusts the project scope and incorporates these new features, demonstrating high adaptability in innovation.
- Resilience: Despite facing technical challenges during the beta testing phase, including server crashes and compatibility issues with certain devices, TechVision's team remains resilient. They address these issues promptly, learning from setbacks and ultimately delivering a stable and well-received product, showcasing resilience in innovation.

Putting it all together, TechVision's "Innovation Momentum" for the fitness tracking app project would be high, reflecting the combination of its fast-paced development process (velocity), ability to adapt to user feedback and market demands (adaptability), and resilience in overcoming technical challenges (resilience). This formula provides a holistic measure of the organization's innovation capability and its ability to drive meaningful change in the market.

Let's assign some hypothetical values to each component of the "Innovation Momentum" formula for better understanding:

Innovation Momentum (IM):

$$IM = Velocity \times Adaptability \times Resilience^2$$

Let's say we're evaluating TechVision's innovation momentum for their fitness tracking app project:

- Velocity: Suppose TechVision's development team manages to conceive and implement new features at a rapid pace. On a scale of 1 to 10, with 10 representing the highest velocity, let's give them a velocity score of 8.

- Adaptability: TechVision is known for its ability to pivot and adapt quickly to market demands. On the same scale, let's assign them a score of 9 for adaptability.
- Resilience: Despite facing technical challenges during the beta testing phase, TechVision's team remains resilient and resolves these issues effectively. On the scale, let's give them a resilience score of 7.

Now, let's plug these values into the formula:

- IM=8×9×49
- IM=3,528

So, TechVision's Innovation Momentum for their fitness tracking app project would be 3,528. This numerical value represents the combined effect of their velocity, adaptability, and resilience in driving innovation forward. The higher the Innovation Momentum, the stronger the organization's ability to innovate and succeed in the market.

To determine the maximum value for the Innovation Momentum (IM) formula, we need to consider the maximum scores for each component: Velocity, Adaptability, and Resilience.

Let's assume that the maximum score for each component is 10, representing the highest possible performance in each area.

Maximum IM=10,000

Therefore, the maximum value for the Innovation Momentum (IM) formula, given our assumptions, is 10,000. This would represent the highest possible level of innovation momentum, where the organization demonstrates exceptional speed, adaptability, and resilience in driving innovation forward.

Here you would notice that I have given high, that is exponential weightage to resilience, this also means their ability to learn from failures.

SpaceX for example is perhaps best known for its resilience. The firm has experienced multiple high-profile failures, such as the initial failed launches of Falcon 1 and the explosion of the Falcon 9 rocket during a test. Despite these setbacks, SpaceX has consistently bounced back, learned from its failures, and achieved groundbreaking successes, including the first privately-funded spacecraft to reach the International Space Station (Dragon) and the development of reusable rockets. Given SpaceX's exceptional ability to recover and improve after failures, SpaceX would get 10 for Resilience in my rating.

Let us now tap into unexplored ways of measuring innovation in your company or university or for self-evaluation. Creating a smartphone app or PC software to measure a person's innovation based on their usage patterns is a novel approach that merges technology with behavioural analysis. By tracking the diversity of applications a person uses, the app can identify a wide range of interests and engagements, indicating a propensity for innovation. For example, individuals who frequently explore emerging technologies, utilize creative tools, and engage in professional networking are likely to exhibit innovative traits. This diversity in app usage suggests a curiosity and willingness to adapt to new tools and methodologies, essential qualities for innovative thinking.

Moreover, the app can monitor educational and developmental activities, providing insights into how committed the user is to continuous learning. By tracking time spent on platforms like Coursera or LinkedIn Learning, as well as engagement with research tools and scientific journals, the app can gauge a person's dedication to acquiring new knowledge and skills. Innovators often stay ahead of the curve by constantly learning and applying new information and such data points can be strong indicators of an individual's innovative potential.

By looking into how much we use apps for getting things done and working together, you will be surprised to learn that it's a super good way to see who's good at figuring things out and who knows how to work nicely with others in projects. People who are good at coming up with fresh ideas also know how to get the team together to make those ideas happen. When we delve into the ways everyone discusses and plans on apps like Slack and Trello, it's easier to spot who's taking charge and who knows how to keep a project on track.

If you mix that with entering into coding battles or solving puzzles, you're really beginning to show who is ready to successfully deal with the fraught material and work well with a team. But, building an app that can look around like that means you must be extremely careful about everyone's privacy. Everyone involved needs the complete picture on what data is getting obtained and what's being done with it. It's all about keeping it clear and getting an okay from the people whose data you're using: the tricks and tools used to sift through all this data need constant updates to keep things fair and avoid playing favourites by accident. Once these hurdles are jumped, the app can serve up some tailor-made tips and spotlight areas where someone could improve their approach in innovating. Wrapping this all up, this bold strategy to gauge who's an innovator could really shake up the way we spot and support the intellectual types in all sorts of arenas.

Measuring the innovativeness of an idea involves evaluating various dimensions that collectively capture its originality, impact, feasibility, and implementation. While it's challenging to reduce such a multi-faceted concept to a single formula, a composite scoring system can be developed. Here's a possible approach:

The Innovation Score (IS) formula is designed to provide a structured and quantitative way to assess the innovativeness of an idea by evaluating its originality, impact, feasibility, and execution. Here's an explanation of how the formula works and a step-by-step example.

Innovation Score (IS) Formula:

$$IS = (W_O \cdot S_O) + (W_I \cdot S_I) + (W_F \cdot S_F) + (W_E \cdot S_E)$$

Where:

- W_O, W_I, W_F, W_E are the weights assigned to each component based on its importance.
- S_O, S_I, S_F, S_E are the scores for Originality, Impact, Feasibility, and Execution, respectively.

Components and Scoring:

1. **Originality (S_O):**

   - **Definition:** Measures how novel and unique the idea is compared to existing solutions.
   - **Scoring (0-10):**

     - 0-2: Idea is common and has many existing solutions.
     - 3-5: Idea has some unique elements but is similar to other solutions.
     - 6-8: Idea is quite unique with few similar solutions.
     - 9-10: Idea is highly original with no similar solutions.

2. **Impact (S_I):**

   - **Definition:** Assesses the potential positive effect of the idea on the target audience or market.
   - **Scoring (0-10):**

     - 0-2: Minimal impact, little value added.
     - 3-5: Moderate impact, solves minor issues.
     - 6-8: Significant impact, solves major issues.
     - 9-10: Transformational impact, creates substantial value or solves critical problems.

3. **Feasibility (S_F):**

   - **Definition:** Evaluates how practical and achievable the idea is given current resources and technology.
   - **Scoring (0-10):**

     - 0-2: Highly impractical, requires technology or resources that don't exist.
     - 3-5: Challenging but possible with significant effort.
     - 6-8: Practical and achievable with available resources and technology.
     - 9-10: Easily implementable with existing resources and technology.

4. **Execution (S_E):**

   - **Definition:** Measures the quality and effectiveness of the implementation plan for the idea.
   - **Scoring (0-10):**

     - 0-2: Poorly defined execution plan, high risk of failure.
     - 3-5: Basic execution plan, moderate risk.
     - 6-8: Well-defined execution plan, low risk.
     - 9-10: Comprehensive and highly effective execution plan, very low risk.

Example Calculation:-

Let's assume we have an idea with the following scores:

- Originality (S_O): 8
- Impact (S_I): 7
- Feasibility (S_F): 6
- Execution (S_E): 9

Assuming equal weights for simplicity, where each component has a weight of 0.25:

$$IS = (0.25 \cdot 8) + (0.25 \cdot 7) + (0.25 \cdot 6) + (0.25 \cdot 9)$$

$$IS = 2 + 1.75 + 1.5 + 2.25$$

$$IS = 7.5$$

The Innovation Score (IS) for this idea would be 7.5 out of 10.

CHAPTER IX

Overcoming Common Barriers to Innovation

People discussing ideas over a table

Overcoming barriers to innovation is crucial for organizations seeking growth and success. These barriers can be daunting, but identifying and addressing them systematically can pave the way for a more innovative and dynamic environment. Let's delve into some common obstacles and strategies to dismantle them. At an individual level it could be something like procrastination, we keep pushing things for later as a result we might end up not innovating.

One significant barrier to innovation is the fear of criticism. This fear can paralyze even the most promising innovation efforts. Many individuals worry about the potential backlash from colleagues or superiors when proposing new ideas. To overcome this barrier, it's essential to embrace failure as a natural part of the innovation process.

For Innovation seekers the most important thing when they conduct innovation competition is a positive and encouraging community and whatever the criticism is it should be constructive. That is the reason you might see many innovation competition even coming up with awards like MVP or most valuable participant who successfully motivates the crowd to innovate more.

To really begin with innovation, it's extremely important that leaders are standing nearby encouraging everyone, they must make sure everyone feels like they matter and that what they say isn't simply disappearing into nothing. By pushing for a space where everyone's happy with speaking up and giving helpful thoughts without fear of getting knocked down, team members are essentially set to be part of making new things happen. Next up, dealing with not really knowing which direction things are going to turn can be nerve-wracking because when we're trying to bring new ideas to life, things aren't always going to go according to plan, to deal with this uncertainty, one may immerse oneself in the knowledge that learning everything possible through research, trying things out on a small scale first, and getting the complete picture on the latest in technology can make the unknown much less frightening; this helps in removing the fear that all this effort might not pay off or could even disaster with climbing the job ladder.

Another fraught bit is the worry about ending up on the wrong steps in the stairway of their career due to starting new and creative projects. To calm these jitters, making a work environment feel like a safe no-judgment zone is very important. If people know trying out new items won't backfire, they'll likely jump more into creative ideas. And you can't only stop there, it's key to let out cheers and give high fives for creative ideas and give a nod to those breakthroughs when thinking about someone's climb up their career ladder. This can rev up everyone to chip in with their creative puzzles pretty enthusiastically. While it's easy to see blundering as a major disappointment, flipping the script to see it as lesson time can open everyone up to not being scared of aiming very high, even if they miss a couple of times. Also, playing the long game is key because creating new inventions isn't a rush job. It's like embarking on a ride that tests your patience and willingness to keep trying along the way, that's how innovation decks are shuffled and reshuffled, pushing the limits and seeing where it all could go.

Lack of Incentives at organization is yet another reason that hampers innovation, anyway a corporate employee working in a company gets salary for the work they do, now if the employee goes over and beyond breaks his or her head and come up with something very innovative, what does the employee get out of it directly. By Implementing reward systems for innovative ideas and successful projects. Recognizing and celebrating innovative efforts plays a crucial role, that is the reason many companies these days have some sort of awards for innovation but almost all of them fail in evaluating the innovations, how they pick innovations, other than by traditional nominations, when the employee does something out of the box, how does the evaluation system know about this, this is something which can be thought through and improved, companies who crack this will foster seeds of Innovation. Corporate hackathons are a great way to evaluate this and that is the reason many companies have internal hackathons but they miss out on day-to-day innovations that miss recognition and encouragement.

Cultural barriers within an organization can significantly impact innovation. A culture that resists change or discourages new ideas can stifle creativity. Promoting inclusivity is a powerful way to overcome this barrier. Encouraging diverse perspectives and ideas can lead to more creative solutions and a more collaborative environment. Breaking down silos is equally important. Cross-functional collaboration should be fostered, as silos hinder the flow of information and impede innovation. Encouraging knowledge sharing across departments can lead to more integrated and innovative solutions.

Structural and process constraints can also impede innovation. Bureaucratic procedures and rigid processes can slow down the pace of innovation. Implementing agile frameworks can help organizations adapt quickly to changing circumstances. Agile methodologies encourage iterative development and flexibility, allowing teams to respond promptly to new information and challenges. Additionally, removing unnecessary bureaucracy and simplifying decision-making processes can streamline innovation efforts, making it easier for ideas to move from conception to execution.

Insufficient Customer Insight is another barrier, the more relevant & valid data you collect from the users the better, this why tech companies are so successful as they know their customers so well that somethings even the customer also may not be aware of themselves.

By Conducting regular market research, gathering customer feedback, and using data analytics to understand customer needs and preferences this barrier can be overcome.

Resource deficiencies can be a significant barrier to innovation. Lack of budget, time, or access to necessary tools and technologies can hinder innovative projects. To a large extent in India this problem is solved by making internet accessible to the masses for a low cost, people have access to technology to learn anything they want.

> *"All of us do not have equal talent. But, all of us have an equal opportunity to develop our talents - Dr. A.P.J. Abdul Kalam"*

At an organization level, to mitigate this barrier, organizations should prioritize innovation by allocating specific budget and time for innovation initiatives. Seeking external partnerships can also provide additional resources and expertise. Collaborating with startups, universities, or other organizations can offer new perspectives and access to cutting-edge technologies and research.

To really get far and succeed, companies need to work together and have a good plan. It's all about not giving up and daring to be different because just wanting to be innovative isn't enough it's of significant consequence that needs everyone in on it, always prepared to make changes and try new ways. And we may thus possibly conclude, if companies foster an environment where people feel supported, celebrate unpredictability, and give power to their workers, they can really start to tap into everything they must offer. Using intelligent and informed moves, they can get past the usual hurdles and grow in an enormous and lasting way.

A boy treating himself with an ice cream

Rewarding yourself for your successes, no matter how small, is crucial for maintaining motivation and a positive mindset. When you acknowledge your achievements with a tangible reward, such as treating yourself to an ice cream or booking a trip, you create a direct link between your efforts and a pleasurable outcome. I always make sure to reward myself, that quite explains why I go in random solo trips all of a sudden sometimes, this is a truly rewarding experience and when you come back after a trip you could come back fresh recharged and help you think better too.

Traveling to new places can indeed enhance innovation and expand your thinking.

You Step Out of Your Comfort Zone, when you visit foreign places, you're exposed to different norms, cultures, and lifestyles. For this to work you should avoid pre-booked tours and packages from agents and tourist companies because if you do this there is no learning or challenges, from airport pickup, to food, to stay everything is taken care by them, you don't have an opportunity to think!

By booking an impromptu trip that is from flight tickets, hotels, places to see, eat and visit, this challenges your existing perspectives and encourages personal growth. Innovation often thrives when we break away from routine and explore the unfamiliar.

Interacting with people from diverse backgrounds fosters creativity. You gain an appreciation for different ways of thinking, problem-solving, and living. These insights can inspire novel ideas and approaches.

Travel exposes you to local customs, traditions, and practices. By travelling to places like Yakutsk, Russia I got a totally different perspective of life in extremely cold weather which is much beyond my normal imagination. Having experienced extremely cold weather myself, when I think out innovation solutions for countries with cold weather, I know what are the possible problems that we are looking at and what could be potential solutions to overcome this. In one innovation challenge we were proposing roads that you could charge cars, so here considering the snow and winter was crucial in shaping the solution. As you immerse yourself in these environments, you absorb unique knowledge and viewpoints. When you return home, you can apply these fresh insights to your work or creative endeavours.

Visiting innovation hubs, attending conferences, or collaborating with experts in different countries allows you to learn from the best. You'll discover cutting-edge technologies, novel business models, and disruptive ideas that can fuel your own innovative thinking.

Travel broadens your horizons, encourages adaptability, and provides a rich tapestry of experiences. These factors contribute to a more innovative mindset, enabling you to think beyond boundaries and create impactful solutions.

This positive reinforcement not only makes the hard work feel worthwhile but also encourages you to continue striving towards your goals. Celebrating your wins, even with small gestures, helps to break the cycle of constant striving and allows you to appreciate the progress you've made, fostering a sense of accomplishment and well-being.

Moreover, taking the time to reward yourself can significantly reduce stress and prevent burnout. In a world where the pace of life is often relentless, and the next challenge is always on the horizon, it's easy to neglect self-care and push through without pause. By consciously deciding to reward yourself, you create moments of respite that allow you to recharge and reflect. These breaks can rejuvenate your energy and enthusiasm, making you more resilient and better equipped to tackle future challenges. In essence, rewarding yourself is an essential practice for sustaining long-term success and maintaining a healthy balance between ambition and self-compassion.

CHAPTER X

Sustainable and Social Innovation

Sustainable and social innovation is all about coming up with ways to tackle big world issues, including changes in the Earth's weather, unfairness in society and the running out of important resources. Instead of just coming up with ideas that will earn money, this approach is planning on finding methods that are good for the planet and people too. Through weaving basic principles into the very heart of how new ideas are born, whether in companies, local governments or neighbourhood groups, positive effects that remain can happen alongside boosting the economy and staying strong during hard times. If you observe closely you will find out that tackling global problems doesn't simply stop at addressing them it's also about nurturing economic health and staying strong through adversity.

The reason I have included this chapter is because there is no other segment I have won most of my innovation awards other than sustainable and social innovation, one of my best innovation challenge wins where I went on to win three innovation awards in a single challenge was in the sustainability sector. Some of the biggest win were also in the sustainability sector, NASA came up with an innovation challenge some time back to come up with innovation to make spacecrafts more sustainable, this is because there is always scope for improvisation and when you improve things if you make things sustainable and make impact in the lives of people, it could be something like making the live of waste sorting worker easy by simplifying his or her work it is a positive impact, so we should always try to come up with optimizations on everything, carry an optimization mindset, this will encourage you to constantly think out new ideas. One of the key aspects of sustainable innovation is its focus on the long-term consequences of development. Traditional innovation often prioritizes short-term gains and market competitiveness, sometimes at the expense of environmental and social well-being. In contrast, sustainable innovation considers the full lifecycle of products and services, from sourcing materials to production processes, and ultimately to disposal or recycling. This holistic approach ensures that every step minimizes negative environmental impacts, reduces waste, and conserves resources, thereby supporting a circular economy. Social innovation, closely related to sustainable innovation, emphasizes the importance of addressing societal needs and challenges through creative solutions. It involves the development of new strategies, concepts, and organizational forms that improve the welfare of individuals and communities. This can include innovations in education, healthcare, housing, and social services that are more accessible, equitable, and efficient. Social innovation often relies on a collaborative approach, bringing together diverse stakeholders, including non-profits, businesses, government agencies, and the communities themselves, to co-create solutions that are contextually relevant and sustainable. A prime example of sustainable and social innovation is the rise of renewable energy technologies. Innovations in solar, wind, and other renewable energy sources have not only provided cleaner alternatives to fossil fuels but have also spurred economic opportunities and improved energy access in underserved regions. For instance, solar microgrids in rural areas of developing countries have enabled communities to have reliable electricity for the first time, empowering them to pursue education, improve healthcare, and enhance their overall quality of life. These renewable energy projects often involve local communities in the planning and implementation stages, ensuring that the solutions are tailored to their specific needs and are sustainable in the long term.

Another notable area of sustainable and social innovation is the development of sustainable agriculture practices. Innovations such as precision farming, vertical gardens, and agroforestry systems have the potential to transform food production, making it more efficient and less harmful to the environment. These practices promote soil health, reduce water usage, and increase crop yields, which are crucial for feeding a growing global population. Additionally, sustainable agriculture can create economic opportunities for small-scale farmers and rural communities, contributing to social stability and reducing poverty.

"Science is a beautiful gift to humanity; we should not distort it - Dr. A.P.J. Abdul Kalam"

Sustainable and social innovation requires a shift in mindset from traditional business and development practices. It involves embracing values such as inclusivity, equity, and environmental stewardship, and recognizing that long-term success is intertwined with the well-being of the planet and its inhabitants. Organizations that prioritize sustainable and social innovation are better positioned to navigate the complexities of the modern world, build resilient communities, and contribute to a more just and sustainable future. As more stakeholders embrace this approach, we can expect to see a proliferation of innovative solutions that not only drive economic growth but also foster a healthier, more equitable world for generations to come.

A lot more innovation scope exists in the field of sustainability in my opinion that will transcend boundaries. Humanity has long sought to bend nature to its will, attempting to manipulate and control the very forces that give us life. But what if instead, we learned to listen? To have a true dialogue with the natural world around us? It sounds like fantasy, but the ability to communicate clearly across the barriers that separate us from other forms of life could be the key innovation that saves our species and our planet.

Imagine being able to convey our needs directly to nature itself - whether that's requesting a timely rain to combat drought, calling forth a gentle breeze to clear choking wildfire smoke, or simply asking a fruit tree to prioritize producing apples over other crops. And in return, to hear and understand nature's own communications to us, its pleas forest and replenishment, its warnings of oncoming disasters. It could fundamentally reshape humanity's relationship with our life-sustaining biosphere.

A boy using technology to request rainfall to extinguish a forest fire

Of course, such communication would not be limited merely to the lifeforms on our own planet. With the ability to translate across vast linguistic and cognitive divides, we could finally engage in dialogue with intelligences across interstellar distances. To share knowledge, culture, and innovations with alien species could open up entire new frontiers of existence and understanding for both sides.

Whether communicating with plants and animals on Earth or cosmic civilizations amongst the stars, bridging these profound gaps is the next great frontier. It could be the innovation that not only saves us, but propels our civilization to heights we can scarcely yet imagine.

"Each individual creature on this beautiful planet is created by God to fulfill a particular role - Dr. A.P.J. Abdul Kalam"

The ability to listen to nature's voice may be what finally allows humanity's own voice to persist across the galactic ages.

A young girl talking to her dogs by translating language across species

We know that even the smallest items such as microorganisms and the largest, like whales, are extremely important to our planet. These tiny helpers aid in making healthy soil by moving nutrients around, which is extremely important for life everywhere. Quickly, bees are in the area, not only flying around but doing something important - pollinating plants which let us have items such as food and oxygen because crops and forests grow. Whales might seem they're just swimming but they're actually keeping the ocean's life in balance by where they what they eat. And it's not only one or two animals, every single creature, big and small, has a meaningful spot in keeping our world going. Since everything, from a tiny bug to the top predator, is hooked into this large life web, we've all got to step up, respect, and look after every living being. Doing that keeps our world great, preventing it from losing its beauty and ensuring it stays amazing for the people who'll be here after us.

CHAPTER XI

Innovation for Content Creators

A content creator looking for ideas

To stand out in a crowded digital space and maintain audience interest, content creators often have to come up with fresh and engaging ideas consistently. The ideation process can be sped up with the use of various tools and techniques. One effective approach is brainstorming. The content creator can get a lot of ideas without having to refine them right away by setting aside time for brainstorming. There are a lot of ways to stimulate creative thinking and see things from new angles, like mind mapping and the SCAMPER method (Substitute, Combine, Adapt, Modify, Put to another use, Eliminate, and Reverse).

Collaborating with other creators can spark new ideas and bring fresh perspectives. Platforms like Collabspace and Influence.co help connect creators for potential collaborations. By working with others, you can create unique content that might not have been possible on your own, tapping into new audiences and creative styles. Collaborating with YouTubers from different niches can breathe new life into your content by infusing it with fresh perspectives and ideas. When you team up with creators who have expertise in areas outside your own, you can explore themes and topics you might not have considered before. For instance, a travel vlogger collaborating with a tech reviewer can create unique content that blends travel experiences with tech gadget reviews, appealing to a broader audience and introducing innovative storytelling techniques. A tech gadget review expert when invited to a travel vlogging channel can recommend various travel related gadgets and tech that can help audience. This cross-niche synergy not only diversifies your content but also keeps your existing audience engaged and excited about what's coming next.

We can also find fresh and exciting content if we collaborate across unexpected niches. For example, a travel and food vlogger might work with a tech influencer to talk about how technology is changing the food and travel industries. If they worked together, they could make a show about robotic chefs, AI-powered restaurant recommendations, and futuristic travel gadgets. A fusion of food, travel, and technology not only broadens audiences, it introduces innovative content that stands out in a crowded market. Such collaborations also provide an opportunity for audience cross-pollination. Working together, you get to tap into each other's audiences since each YouTuber brings their own audience. With mutual exposure, you can get new subscribers who wouldn't have discovered your channel otherwise. As viewers enjoy seeing their favourite creators come together, the combined fan bases often mean higher engagement rates. In addition to getting more likes, comments, and shares for your content, collaborating with YouTubers across different niches helps you learn and grow. Each creator brings unique skills, techniques, and insights to their content, so by observing their creative process, you can learn new ways to make your own content better. Whether it's mastering a new editing style, understanding different audience engagement strategies, or learning how to market your videos, these collaborations can be incredibly beneficial. Not only does this exchange of knowledge improve your content, but it keeps you ahead of trends and keeps you innovating.

A real-time connection and community can be created by leveraging live interactive content. Viewers could ask questions, suggest dishes, and even vote on what the vlogger should cook next, as the travel and food vlogger hosts live cooking sessions. You can add AR overlays to these live interactions to learn more about the ingredients, cultural context, and cooking techniques. Not only does this make the content more dynamic and engaging, but it also fosters a deeper connection with the audience, since they feel directly involved.

Tools like BuzzSumo, Google Trends, adwords keyword explorer and AnswerThePublic provide insights into what topics are currently trending and what questions people are asking. By analysing popular content and trending searches, you can identify hot topics and niches that your audience is interested in, inspiring new vlog ideas. Look at successful YouTubers in the same area as you and figure out how you can make their content ideas your own without just copying them. Instead, let their videos spark your own creative thoughts. It's all about seeing what unique touch you can bring. When looking at their most viewed videos, you should think carefully about the topics they're covering and think of ways you could do things differently. Using tools like Hootsuite, Sprout Social, and Brandwatch, you can watch what is happening on social media.

This is a wonderful way to pick up on what interests your viewers and other big names are discussing. Digging into social media to notice these conversations and trends helps you identify what might inspire your next idea. And doing some homework on content is really helpful, too. By looking at what's trending, learning what formats viewers are into, and getting the details on what they like, you can get several insights. Tools such as Google

Trends, BuzzSumo, and looking at social media stats help you catch onto hot topics and formats that win audiences over. It's a clever move for creating material that grasps attention while making it unmistakably yours. You can also gather fresh content ideas by getting your audience to help out. Running contests or asking for their content, such as video submissions, adds to your content calendar with new material, making them feel special and closer to your channel because you're celebrating their contributions. And in the final analysis, one finds that by encouraging viewers to join in and tracking what's currently becoming very popular, you manage to keep your content both fresh and connected with what people want to see. Keeping your content relevant and engaging isn't only about chasing trends; it's also about making sure it mirrors what your audience wholly enjoys while making it authentically you.

You might have seen some popular youtubers making videos out of comments shared by the viewers in various videos this also is a good way to create new content for videos.

Engaging with the audience is another powerful technique for idea generation. Content creators can utilize polls, Q&A sessions, and feedback forms to understand their audience's preferences, questions, and interests. Platforms like Instagram Stories, YouTube Community, and Twitter polls allow for direct interaction with followers, providing a wealth of ideas based on real audience needs and desires. This not only helps in creating content that is highly relevant but also fosters a sense of community and engagement with the audience.

Leveraging technology and AI-powered tools can also significantly enhance the ideation process. Tools like ChatGPT, Jasper, and Copy.ai can generate content ideas, suggest headlines, and even create draft content based on specific inputs. These AI tools can serve as creative partners, offering new angles and concepts that might not have been considered otherwise. Additionally, content creators can use visual inspiration tools like Pinterest and Canva's design templates to spark ideas for visually-driven content, such as infographics, videos, and social media posts.

Content that highlights sustainability and social impact can resonate strongly with modern audiences. Showcase eco-friendly travel tips, sustainable cooking practices, or local initiatives making a positive impact. This not only raises awareness but also aligns your content with values that are increasingly important to viewers.

A great way to get new ideas is to repurpose existing content. Take a popular blog post, podcast episode or an old video and reformat it into something else. A blog post could be turned into a video tutorial, or a long video could be broken down into a series of shorter clips. By doing this, you're reaching new audiences and maximizing the value of your existing content.

I was thinking about various ways in which Vloggers and content creators can think out various content ideas for their videos, that is when I got this idea of different pathways based on their mood and interest that the viewers can choose these various combinations and pathways can create new content in various different ways that was not there before let me explain this in detail.

Creating a short movie or vlog with multiple endings, where viewers can choose their own path, is a highly engaging and innovative way to captivate your audience. The interactive format lets viewers control what happens in the story based on how they feel and what they're interested in. It's like a short movie with five possible endings: one could be horrible or tragic, another could be happy, one could be ambiguous, one could be twisty. Start by outlining the story so that it branches into multiple paths. If the vlogger is doing a food and travel vlog, it might start when he or she arrives in a new city. They could choose between different activities or culinary experiences. Think about a storyline where the vlogger is exploring a vibrant city, and he's deciding whether to check out a historic temple or a bustling local market. The choices you make should offer unique experiences and set the stage for future choices, creating a rich tapestry of narratives.

Identify key decision points in the story where viewers will choose what happens next. In videos or vlogs this can be shown as related videos or QR codes which they can scan to branch out to next video in a series, this will create different pathways but the idea is prepare the content pathways in such a way that even if people choose different pathways the content makes sense.

I could watch Video 1, then either of the video 2.a, video 2.b, video 2.c, video 2.d and come back to video 3. Here we have many pathways, this is just an idea to give an understanding of the concept.

- **Video 1 – Video 2.a – Video 3 could be path -1**
- **Video 1 – Video 2.b – Video 3 could be path -2**
- **Video 1 – Video 2.c – Video 3 could be path -3**
- **Video 1 – Video 2.d – Video 3 could be path -4**
- **Video 1 – Video 2.e – Video 3 could be path -5**

For your project, now you have this idea where viewers can choose what they want to do next with the video they are watching like deciding to enter into a cooking class with a chef or maybe sit on a rooftop and enjoy some food. Everywhere they click leads them down a different path, and there is a profound and deep-seated certainty that these choices will keep them hooked. It's your job to map out these different routes, each with its own story, making sure they start, hustle through the middle, and end in a way that feels complete on its own yet magically fits into the larger picture. You need to sketch out the scenarios for wherever their choices might take them. If the story branches out to a local market adventure versus a detour through ancient ruins, you're going to capture both and whatever might come after. When writing, make sure each option leads to something they'll remember choosing different places, maybe odd characters, reconfiguring the tenor or how you deliver the story, keeping it interesting; then there's the heavyweight task of keeping the whole show on the road, continuity-wise. If one moment, a character's relaxing in one scene and then appears in another choice looking different or acting out of sync, it's going to throw the audience off. Plan to keep your backdrop, the gear, and any get-up consistent, this precision in the details knits the story's fabric, letting viewers swerve paths without tripping up the narrative's flow.

Dunk every choice they make into a storyline that feels personal and fully rounded, guiding it back to the heart of the tale. And you might have heard that the devil is in the details, so you're locking down everything from scripts for each twist and turn to making sure a scene shot Tuesday can hand off smoothly to another filmed two weeks later. Shine a special, rare light on each option to keep the individuals watching and guessing.

Use annotations, cards, or end screens on platforms like YouTube to enable interactivity. These tools allow viewers to click and choose the next part of the story. Set up the video on a platform that supports these interactive features effectively. On YouTube, use the end screen feature to link to the next video in each pathway. Make sure each choice is clearly presented and easy for viewers to navigate, enhancing the interactive experience.

Edit each pathway separately, ensuring that transitions between choices are smooth. Create a master video that includes all the decision points where viewers will make their choices. The editing process should focus on creating a seamless flow between segments, so the viewer's transition from one scene to the next feels natural and intuitive. This involves precise cuts and possibly adding narrative elements that help bridge the choices. Ensure that each choice links to the correct video segment and test the navigation thoroughly to make sure it works flawlessly. The goal is to make the interactive experience as smooth and engaging as possible, reducing any friction that might disrupt the viewer's immersion.

Promote the interactive video on social media, encouraging viewers to explore different pathways and share their experiences. Ask them to comment on their favourite choices and endings, fostering a community discussion around the various pathways. This engagement not only increases viewer interaction but also helps you understand which storylines resonate most with your audience. Engaging with your audience in this way can provide valuable feedback and ideas for future interactive projects.

By providing multiple endings and pathways, you create a unique, engaging experience that invites viewers to become part of the storytelling process. You'll get more viewers engaged and set your content apart in a crowded digital market. You can deepen audience connection with interactive storytelling, providing a novel viewing experience that keeps people coming back. You can also experiment with different narrative possibilities and viewer preferences in real-time with it.

Content creators can significantly enhance their storytelling and viewer engagement by innovating with camera perspectives. One compelling method is using a first-person perspective, which immerses viewers in the creator's experience. This technique is particularly effective in travel vlogs, adventure sports, and gaming content. For instance, a travel vlogger might use a head-mounted camera to capture their exploration of a bustling marketplace. Viewers experience the journey as if they are there, seeing everything from haggling with vendors to sampling street food, which creates a highly engaging and personal experience.

To get stunning aerial views that would otherwise be impossible to capture, drones are another innovative approach. Adding a dramatic and visually appealing element to your content is easy with this perspective, whether it's landscapes, cities, or large-scale events. A food and travel vlogger might start a video with a sweeping drone shot of a scenic coastal town, then zoom in to show off the restaurant they're going to. By using 360-degree video, you can enhance viewer engagement by offering a fully immersive experience. This technique sets a captivating scene right from the beginning. In this format, viewers can choose their own viewing angle, so it's perfect for virtual tours, behind-the-scenes stuff, and interactive stories. During a food festival, a vlogger could use a 360-degree camera to capture the whole environment, allowing viewers to navigate the scene themselves. It lets them choose which stalls or activities they want to focus on, so they feel like they're there and get involved.

For instance, such as about a travel video showing how a beach changes from morning to night. They could do it very quickly with a time-lapse, making it really interesting to see the whole day go by in just a short clip. Or imagine a food expert who's creating something truly unique. Instead of watching every single moment of several hours, you get to see the magic happen in just a couple of minutes through a fast forward video: these tricks, called time-lapse and stop-motion, are of significant consequence for people making spectacular videos. What they do is they pack up a long period into a quick video that's really exciting, imagine seeing a whole day zipping by as the sun sets, or cars zooming on streets, or even showing how busy a kitchen can get. All of this makes for videos that hold your attention because there's always something changing or moving. By focusing on key moments and shifts, the reader is destined to learn that these techniques aren't simply about speeding things up or making things look busy, they're about giving a fresh perspective on things that take time, like watching a location come alive or a meal being made from scratch.

Split screen technique

A split-screen technique can simultaneously show different perspectives or actions happening at the same time. You might have come across such reels in platforms like Instagram where two people holding their selfie camera bump into each other and the final video will contain and split screen of two perspectives, this is another way of creating new content which is interesting for the viewers because they have not usually used to seeing content from both the perspective together.

You might have seen various content across social media that gets viral from time to time, let me try to give you a very simple formula to start with which can measure if your content has the potential to be viral.

To predict the viral potential of a video or a content before it is posted, we need to focus on factors that can be assessed without actual engagement metrics. Here we are assuming no followers and zero influence of algorithms. That means we are measuring the viral potential of content irrespective of the influence of the social media account used for posting, this is necessary for the sake of simplicity.

So, these factors can include the quality, uniqueness, and elements of the content that typically contribute to virality. Here's a simplified predictive model based on pre-posting criteria:

Factors to Consider

- **Content Quality (CQ):-** A subjective score based on the technical quality of the video, such as audio, video, editing, and overall production value, rated from 1 to 10.
- **Originality (O):-** A subjective score based on how unique and innovative the content is compared to other content in the platform, rated from 1 to 10.
- **Emotional Appeal (EA):-** A subjective score based on the emotional impact of the video (e.g., humor, inspiration, shock value), rated from 1 to 10.
- **Trend Relevance/Repeatability (TR):-** A score based on how well the video aligns with current trends or viral themes, rated from 1 to 10. If the content has something that would prompt user to repeat something unique with ease, then it should be scored higher.

- **Audience Fit (AF):-** A score indicating how well the video fits the interests of a larger audience, rated from 1 to 10. If the content can be appealing to a kid as well as grandmother that is wide age group, gender, demography then this score will be high.

Simplified Predictive Formula

We will create a formula that combines these factors with equal weights for simplicity. Adjustments can be made based on specific priorities.

$$VII = \frac{CQ + O + EA + TR + AF}{5}$$

Steps to Use the Formula

- Evaluate Each Factor: Rate the video on a scale of 1 to 10 for each of the five factors:
- Content Quality (CQ), Originality (O), Emotional Appeal (EA), Trend Relevance (TR), Audience Fit (AF)
- Calculate the VII: Sum the scores and divide by 5.
- Example Calculation:Suppose you evaluate a video as follows:
- Content Quality (CQ): 8
- Originality (O): 7
- Emotional Appeal (EA): 9
- Trend Relevance (TR): 6
- Audience Fit (AF): 8

Calculate the VII:

$$VII = \frac{8 + 7 + 9 + 6 + 8}{5} = \frac{38}{5} = 7.6$$

Interpretation

- A higher VII indicates a higher potential for the video to go viral.
- Set a threshold based on historical data or expert opinion to determine if a video is likely to be viral (e.g., a VII above 7 might indicate high viral potential).

This simplified formula provides a way to predict the viral potential of a video before posting by focusing on key qualitative aspects. It is easy to use and adjust, making it a practical tool for creators and marketers aiming to maximize their content's impact. Here if you ask me the most important factor is Trend Relevance/ Repeatability which I would call the viral sauce.

Videos often become viral and set trends when they feature unique, memorable elements that resonate deeply with audiences, encouraging widespread sharing and imitation. This virality is driven by the combination of originality, emotional appeal, and cultural relevance. For instance, the scene in the movie Pushpa where the protagonist's slipper falls off, paired with the catchy "Srivelli" dance, became a viral sensation. Its uniqueness lies in the simple yet impactful visual of a falling slipper and the infectious dance moves, which viewers found easy to recreate and share. The scene's humor, combined with its relatability and catchy beat, made it a cultural touchstone, inspiring countless memes, dance challenges, and social media posts. This phenomenon illustrates how a single, well-crafted moment can transcend its original context to become a trend-setting cultural icon, enabling users to adopt and adapt the style as their own. The makers of the Pushpa movie had got concept very well and they have incorporated many such moves throughout the songs of next version of the movie with steps like the inverted tea spin dance move which also went viral was trending in Youtube at a point.

For the sake of my international audience who might not have heard of the above example, let me include few more examples which were very popular, this would help you understand what I am referring to better.

- **Gangnam Style by Psy:-** The music video for "Gangnam Style" became a global sensation in 2012 due to its catchy music, quirky dance moves (like the horse-riding dance), and humorous imagery. The dance moves were easy to imitate and became a widespread trend, with celebrities, politicians, and people worldwide creating their own versions.
- **The Ice Bucket Challenge:-** This viral campaign in 2014 involved participants dumping buckets of ice water over their heads to raise awareness and funds for ALS research. It spread rapidly on social media due to its simple yet engaging challenge format, encouraging people to participate, nominate others, and donate to the cause.
- **Baby Shark Dance:-** If you just look at the lyrics and number of views of this song you would not need any more examples on Trend Relevance/Repeatability, the children's song "Baby Shark" by Pinkfong gained immense popularity in 2018 due to its catchy melody, repetitive lyrics, and accompanying dance moves that were easy for young children to mimic. The song's infectious nature led to a global dance craze, spawning numerous viral videos and challenges.

Personal growth and continuous learning are really important if you want to keep coming up with new ideas. Content creators need to delve into expanding their knowledge and skills by doing items such as taking courses, going to workshops, and reading a lot. When they learn about new material, techniques, and different subjects, it can give them a lot of amazing knowledge and ways to make their content. There's a location online where you can find a large amount of different courses - Coursera, Skillshare, and MasterClass are a few of them. These platforms have courses that not only teach you hands-on skills but also can inspire your imagination. If content creators stay open and curious about learning new things, there is unsurprisingly a potential to keep their creativity flowing and keep making things that catch people's attention.

CHAPTER XII

Steps the Common Man Can Take to Accelerate Innovation in the Country

The Government of India began something wonderful called MyGov website, and it's really making a big difference when it comes to coming up with new ideas in the country. This platform is the messenger between ordinary people and the higher-ups, letting everyone have a shot at shaping the nation, at the beginning, the marvellous part about this government website is that it lets anyone include their ideas on big issues through items such as discussion online, voting in polls, and participating in innovation competitions. This all comes together to really understand the ideas and imagination flowing, allowing people from all walks of life to join forces and tackle some pretty big concerns that we're all facing. But, there's more: Mygov.in doesn't stop there, it offers challenges, contests, and even games like quizzes. This is a master brewer way of giving people a push to think outside the box and submit solutions to the government that not only make sense but can actually be used in real life. By bringing together a large group of ideas from different brains, the website MyGov manages to uncloak the details on how to get past obstacles in various sectors.

This site isn't only about throwing ideas around, it also connects ordinary citizens directly with the people leading the nation, making sure what you think or suggest doesn't end up in a forgotten email folder. By breaking down the walls for forums and getting feedback through different sessions, it makes sure actions taken are actually in tune with what people need and want. That means policy doesn't simply sound good on paper but works in real life, making everything better for everyone. On another note, MyGov.in is also this amazing library stacked with information, data, and tips on everything making it the primary for using brain power and starting actions into high gear in local communities, it's making people smarter and sharper, lighting fires beneath people to start constructing, mending and bettering their surroundings on their terms.

To wrap it all up in a neat package, MyGov.in is more or less igniting a revolution of thought and action in India. It's creating this great combination of dialogue, teamwork, clear-cut dealings, and learning sessions elevating everyone involved and inching India closer to being not only innovative but inclusively innovative. Standing on the superpowers of technology and people power, MyGov.in is ready for revving up India onto a fast lane towards renovation and all-round growth.

1. People can make various types of contributions using MyGov.in, spanning from sharing ideas and feedback to actively participating in contests and initiatives. Here are some ways individuals can contribute to the platform.
2. Users can share innovative ideas and suggestions on a wide range of topics, including governance, policy reforms, social issues, and community development. These ideas can be submitted through open forums or specific discussions initiated by government departments or ministries.
3. MyGov.in provides a platform for citizens to provide feedback and suggestions on government policies, programs, and initiatives. Users can participate in online consultations, surveys, and polls to share their opinions and recommendations directly with policymakers.
4. MyGov.in regularly organizes contests, challenges, and hackathons on various themes and issues. Citizens can participate in these initiatives by submitting their innovative solutions, designs, or proposals to address specific challenges posed by the government or partnering organizations.
5. The platform facilitates citizen engagement in the policymaking process by inviting inputs and insights on draft policies and legislation. Users can review policy documents, provide

comments, and suggest revisions to help shape the final outcomes.

6. MyGov.in encourages citizens to volunteer for social and community service initiatives. Users can join volunteer groups, participate in cleanliness drives, tree plantation campaigns, and other community-based activities to contribute to social welfare and environmental conservation efforts.

7. Users can support government campaigns and advocacy efforts by spreading awareness about important issues and initiatives through social media, sharing informative content, and mobilizing community support for key causes.

8. MyGov.in provides a platform for citizens to share success stories, case studies, and best practices from their local communities. These stories highlight innovative solutions, grassroots initiatives, and exemplary efforts that can inspire others and drive positive change.

9. The platform hosts digital dialogues, webinars, and virtual town halls on various topics of public interest. Citizens can participate in these interactive sessions, ask questions, and engage in discussions with policymakers, subject matter experts, and thought leaders.

10. MyGov.in encourages active civic engagement by providing opportunities for citizens to participate in governance processes, including local governance, urban planning, and public service delivery. Users can contribute ideas, suggestions, and feedback to improve governance at the grassroots level.

11. MyGov.in promotes digital literacy and skills development by providing educational resources, tutorials, and online courses on topics such as digital literacy, cybersecurity, and emerging technologies. Users can enhance their digital skills and knowledge through these resources, empowering themselves to adapt to the digital age.

MyGov.in offers a wide range of avenues for citizens to contribute to governance, innovation, and community development, empowering them to play an active role in shaping the future of the nation.

I would give you another example with USA where people there can directly contribute and accelerate innovation in their country, other countries also may have such portals which can be explored by the audience based on their geography. My primarily audience at the time of writing this book was India because I am based out of India and I can better comment out based on ground reality rather than only facts and figures, also by taking example of India I can cover one-sixth of the world's population.

Challenge.gov, much like MyGov.in, serves as a platform for crowdsourcing innovative solutions to various challenges faced by government agencies and organizations in the United States. Here are some ways in which people can contribute using Challenge.gov

1. Challenge.gov hosts a wide range of challenges, competitions, and prize competitions initiated by federal agencies, departments, and other organizations. Participants can submit their solutions, ideas, or proposals to address specific problems and compete for prizes, grants, or recognition.

2. Individuals can contribute innovative solutions to challenges across diverse sectors, including healthcare, energy, environment, education, and public safety. These challenges may range from developing new technologies and products to designing policies and programs aimed at addressing pressing societal issues.

3. Challenge.gov provides a platform for collaboration and networking among participants, government agencies, industry experts, and stakeholders. Participants can connect with others, form teams, and leverage collective expertise to develop comprehensive and impactful solutions.

4. Participants can receive feedback and evaluation from challenge sponsors, judges, and peers throughout the submission process. This feedback helps refine and improve solutions, ensuring they meet the needs and requirements of the challenge.

5. Challenge.gov recognizes and rewards outstanding contributions and innovative solutions through various awards, prizes, and honors. Winning submissions may receive financial rewards, grants, contracts, or opportunities for further development and implementation.

6. Challenge.gov promotes public engagement and transparency by providing information about ongoing challenges, submission guidelines, evaluation criteria, and results. This transparency fosters trust and accountability in the challenge process and encourages broader participation from the public.

7. Participating in challenges on Challenge.gov allows individuals to build their capacity and develop valuable skills such as problem-solving, critical thinking, collaboration, and communication. These skills are transferable and can benefit participants in their careers and personal endeavours.

8. Challenge.gov contributes to building a vibrant innovation ecosystem by bringing together diverse stakeholders, including government agencies, businesses, academia, nonprofit organizations, and citizens. This collaborative approach fosters a culture of innovation and entrepreneurship, driving positive change and societal impact.

9. Challenge.gov promotes the use of open data and open innovation principles by encouraging the sharing of data, ideas, and solutions in the public domain. This open and inclusive approach facilitates knowledge sharing, collaboration, and co-creation of solutions to complex challenges.

10. Challenge.gov facilitates continuous improvement and learning by capturing lessons learned, best practices, and success stories from past challenges. This knowledge sharing enables participants to learn from each other's experiences and apply insights to future challenges, driving ongoing innovation and excellence.

Challenge.gov provides a valuable platform for individuals to contribute their ideas, expertise, and creativity to solve complex challenges and advance innovation in the United States. Through collaboration, transparency, recognition, and skills development, Challenge.gov empowers citizens to make meaningful contributions to the public good and shape the future of their communities and country.

Another thing that we can do is, being an active part of the feedback loop is crucial for driving innovation in any country. As a user of various products and services, you hold valuable insights into what works well and what could be improved. By regularly engaging with the products, you use and paying attention to the details, you can provide specific, actionable feedback. This feedback is essential because it helps companies understand the real-world applications of their products and identify areas that need refinement. When you notice a feature that could be improved or encounter a problem, sharing your experiences can directly influence the development and enhancement of these products.

Understanding and utilizing the appropriate feedback channels can amplify the impact of your input. Many companies have official channels, such as dedicated feedback forms on their websites, customer service contact points, and social media platforms. Engaging in community forums or user groups can also be effective, as these platforms often aggregate feedback from multiple users, highlighting common issues and potential improvements. By providing specific and constructive feedback through these channels, you ensure that your voice is heard and that companies receive the detailed information they need to make meaningful changes.

Public platforms, like social media and review sites, offer another powerful avenue for providing feedback. Sharing your thoughts and experiences on platforms such as Twitter, Facebook, and Google Reviews not only reaches the company but also informs other potential users. This public visibility can pressure companies to respond and make necessary adjustments promptly. Additionally, participating in beta testing programs and customer surveys allows you to give feedback before products are widely released, contributing to a smoother launch and better user experience for everyone.

Ultimately, the role of the consumer in the feedback loop cannot be overstated. By consistently providing thoughtful, respectful, and constructive feedback, you become an integral part of the innovation process. Your input helps companies stay attuned to customer needs and adapt quickly to changing demands. Moreover, fostering a culture of feedback and innovation within your community can drive broader systemic changes, encouraging more companies to prioritize user feedback in their development processes. This collaborative effort between consumers and companies is what propels continuous improvement and innovation, benefiting the entire country.

Let me explain this with an example and different personas, let us assume you have an idea of adding a glow in the dark sticker or illuminating light near the insertion hole of the seat belt of the car this will allow you to easily buckle up the seat belt at night. Now this feature is not there in most of the cars and you would like to bring this innovation to the market that could end up saving a life because as you are aware seat belt plays a crucial role in deciding the fate of the passenger during an accident.

1. Scenario 1:- You go to a local workshop and explain the requirement to the local mechanic and he adds this feature in your car, from then on whoever takes a ride in your car notices this functionality or feature and being an useful feature, gets it implemented in their car and ultimately this trend and requirement get spotted by an automobile manufacturer and they implement it in standard car. The moral of this incident is that individual ideas and grassroots innovations can spark significant changes and improvements in larger systems and industries. By sharing your innovative idea and getting it implemented at a local level, you can create a ripple effect that leads to widespread adoption and potentially life-saving advancements.

2. Scenario 2:- You decide to share your innovative feature on social media, showcasing how it works and explaining its benefits. Your post gains traction, and soon many people are sharing and discussing it. Influencers and bloggers pick up on your idea, and it becomes a hot topic in online communities. This widespread visibility catches the attention of car manufacturers, who start to receive requests from customers wanting this feature. Recognizing the market demand and the safety benefits, manufacturers incorporate it into their designs.

3. Scenario 3:- You take a more formal approach by reaching out to car safety advocacy groups and industry forums, presenting your idea as a potential safety improvement. Your proposal garners support from safety experts and gains attention within the industry. Car manufacturers, always looking for ways to enhance safety features and attract safety-conscious consumers, decide to test and eventually adopt your innovation in their future models.

4. Scenario 4:- You decide to take your idea to the next level by starting a small business. You develop a kit that can be easily installed in any car and start selling it online. Your product quickly gains popularity due to its practical benefits and affordable price. Car enthusiasts and safety-conscious drivers start purchasing your kit, and positive reviews spread across various platforms. Eventually, larger companies notice the demand and approach you for partnerships or to buy your patent, leading to your innovation becoming a standard feature in new cars.

5. Scenario 5:- As an engineer, you recognize the potential of your idea and decide to patent the concept of the glow-in-the-dark or illuminated seat belt insertion point. With the patent secured, you present your idea to several automotive companies, highlighting the safety benefits and potential for market

differentiation. Impressed by your foresight and the documented advantages, a major car manufacturer licenses your patent and integrates the feature into their vehicle designs, promoting it as a new safety enhancement in their marketing campaigns.

6. Scenario 6:- You collaborate with a research institution to conduct a study on the effectiveness of illuminated seat belt insertion points in reducing the time it takes for passengers to buckle up, especially in low-light conditions. The study shows significant improvements in buckling times and overall safety. The findings are published in a reputable journal, garnering attention from the automotive industry and safety regulators. As a result, manufacturers and policymakers consider incorporating this feature as part of new car safety standards.

7. Scenario 7:- You are a respected figure in your local community and use your influence to advocate for this safety feature. You organize community meetings and collaborate with local car clubs, driving schools, and safety organizations to raise awareness about the benefits of illuminated seat belt insertion points. Through persistent advocacy and demonstrations, your idea gains traction, leading to local car dealerships offering the feature as an optional upgrade. Over time, this local movement attracts media attention, leading to broader adoption.

8. Scenario 8:- As a teacher, you introduce the concept of this safety feature to your students as a class project on innovation and engineering. The students develop prototypes and conduct surveys to gather feedback from the community. Their enthusiasm and hard work lead to a well-documented case study, which you present at educational conferences. The project gains recognition, and industry professionals see the value in your students' work, leading to partnerships with schools and further development of the idea.

9. Scenario 9:- You launch a crowdfunding campaign to develop and produce a DIY kit for the illuminated seat belt feature. Your campaign video goes viral, showcasing the ease of installation and the safety benefits. The campaign raises more funds than expected, allowing you to produce the kits on a larger scale. The success of the crowdfunding campaign attracts media attention and highlights consumer interest, prompting automotive companies to take notice and consider incorporating the feature into their future models.

10. Scenario 10:- You decide to share your idea and design specifications on an open-source platform, encouraging other innovators and car enthusiasts to collaborate and improve upon it. This collaborative approach leads to rapid development and enhancement of the feature, with various versions being tested and refined by a community of innovators. The open-source project gains popularity, and automotive companies start adopting the best versions, integrating the feature into their cars as a standard safety enhancement.

I can give you 100 scenarios on how your action can translate your ideas or innovation into reality, the key is to act and you should believe in your idea or innovation and continuously refine it to fill the gaps or drawbacks.

Each scenario highlights different pathways through which an individual's innovative idea can lead to widespread change, demonstrating the power of community, collaboration, and persistence in driving innovation. The core idea is the same: an individual's simple, practical innovation can lead to significant change when shared and adopted by others. This underscores the importance of grassroots innovation and how small ideas, when effectively communicated and shared, can lead to widespread, impactful improvements. The moral is clear: don't underestimate the power of your ideas. By taking action and sharing them, you can contribute to a culture of continuous improvement and innovation, ultimately making a positive difference in the world.

Micro investing can significantly boost innovation in India by democratizing access to capital for startups and small businesses. Unlike angel investing, which often involves substantial sums and sophisticated investors, micro investing allows everyday individuals to contribute smaller amounts to innovative ventures. This approach broadens the investment base, encouraging a diverse array of investors to support early-stage companies. By pooling resources from a larger number of small investors, startups can access the necessary funding to develop and bring innovative ideas to market, fostering a more dynamic and inclusive entrepreneurial ecosystem.

Couple of days ago I came across this unique idea from an Instagram user who uses black and white photographs of weddings and then enhances them with colourful thread to make the flowers popup to create truly innovative piece of art. It adds such a personal touch to the memories captured in those photos. And the fact that these videos are being shared on Instagram shows that there's already an audience appreciating this artistry.

Now, transforming this hobby project into a scalable small business with the help of micro investments could be a game-changer. Imagine being able to hire more hands to assist with the sewing, expanding the reach of this craft to more weddings, events, and perhaps even other types of photography. With additional funds, you could invest in marketing efforts to showcase your unique service to a wider audience, attracting more clients and creating more jobs in the process.

Micro investments from individuals who appreciate the artistry and potential impact of this endeavour could fuel its growth. These investments wouldn't need to be large sums, but rather smaller contributions or access to resources from multiple supporters who believe in the vision and want to be a part of its journey. It's a beautiful example of how community support and collaboration can drive innovation and job creation, even in what started as a simple hobby. One way to take this project larger is by coming up with amazing ideas such as hosting workshops or making DIY kits, this is for people who want to put their own spin to creativity. This might really help the business grow by bringing in more money and making sure it remains for the long haul. It also gives people a chance to demonstrate their creative side and say something about who they are through art.

One thing you should understand is that this it isn't simply about spending lots of money it's much more. We're all about supporting dreams, creativity, and doing things that can really make a difference. When we back projects like this, we're not simply helping them get larger, we're making our towns and places rich in culture and money. It's a scoreboard where everyone's winning, and it begins by getting that even small amounts of money might well end up in large changes.

CHAPTER XIII

How to Organize a Successful Hackathon or Innovation Competition in the Modern Era of AI

The first step is to find out the purpose of the hackathon, it could be for any purpose like to collect new market trends, to just to get some PR and publicity, over the years by posting opportunities at Givemechallenge I have seen a wide variety of objectives.

Once I have submitted ideas to a competition by an automobile giant only to find out later that they were not looking for implementing the ideas but they were looking for various trends in the market, around 500+ ideas were submitted by participants in few days for a crowdsourcing competition and the time taken to announce the winner was only a day, that is when I have figured out they were just looking for current trends in the automobile market.

There was also one leading dish wash manufacturer that was looking for various consumer pain points but the competition was organized to find new product ideas, the management was drilling down to identify the real problems the customers were facing, then rank it and then come up with solutions for the same in existing products, instead of creating something completely new.

Planning a wonderful game or a competition for creating new ideas isn't easy at all, you must know exactly what you have the sincere intention to achieve with the event first. Is it about solving a hard problem, coming up with different business ideas or getting a community interested in new ideas? The hermetic result of this is all tied to a well-thought-out organization, smartly putting plans into action, and truly knowing the creative undercurrents flowing.

I endeavour to elucidate how important it is to know what you want to achieve with your event, this makes sure you get the right people to come and lays down the feeling for the whole notion.

It's also about making sure everything and everyone, such as the money, helpers, and those supporting us, lines up with what we're trying to do, keeping everyone on the same page.

With the advancement of AI there are a variety of ways in which we can leverage AI to improve the user experience and effectiveness of innovation competition and hackathon.

We can Implement AI-driven chatbots to guide participants through the registration process, answer common questions, and handle FAQs. Use AI to match participants with similar interests, skills or project ideas to form balanced and effective teams. Implement AI systems to provide instant feedback on project ideas or prototypes, highlighting strengths and areas for improvement, this can be very useful in avoiding duplicate idea submission which is a big problem in crowdsourcing innovation competitions, also this will help ideas from staying focused on the goals of the challenge.

With some wonderful AI technologies, we can look at how much everyone likes it on different places online, such as social media and messaging apps and make changes quickly to keep things interesting. Also, by putting AI to work on what people are saying as the event happens, we can take as a definite certainty that we'll be catching problems fast and fixing them quickly.

To be honest, I consider choosing the right innovation platform extremely important if you want to get those ideas going and where people can really work together well. You need to make sure everyone has the technology items they need and there's enough room for everybody to either convene in groups or have some alone time to think, the feeling should be happy and motivating. You must balance the hard grind with restful periods and some relaxed social time. Bringing in some experienced people to speak or give advice can help everyone understand better and be very helpful for everyone there.

In any project, mentors are extremely important because they help teams navigate the difficult process of coming up with ideas and building things. They have a lot of experience and know many details that can really change the industry for a team. At first, I didn't think mentors were all that necessary. I learned about how amazing they are a bit late. But, after getting a firsthand in a big challenge, how a mentor guided us all the way to winning, I suddenly understood. We couldn't have won without the Mentor and in the final analysis, we found that the mentor's guidance is of the highest importance.

In our endless pursuit to understand and simplify, the role of mentors can't be overstated. They're our main helpers for everything difficult and smart, figuring out the hard problems, finding easy paths through them, and keeping us from making big mistakes. They ask really good and hard questions that make us think really hard, which kicks our creative gears into overdrive. I've had this mentor once, felt like they were playing the devil's advocate, always challenging ideas, and making sure I got my proposal straight. And when they thought I was ready, they'd include me in the deepest regions, having me pitch my ideas to their well-connected peers, getting all sorts of feedback and readying me for the larger industry. Mentors do more than just intelligent and informed talk, though they keep the team spirit high, pulling us through the ups and downs with eyes on the prize.

Mentor guiding a group during a hackathon

Mentors do a whole lot more than just give advice. They're your ticket to understanding all those confusing market trends and what customers really want. Also, they make sure whatever you dream up during the project isn't only marvelous but actually works in the area in the real world. They even help polish up your team's speed talk and make sure your final show-and-tell grasps everyone's attention. After the event ends, they don't simply disappear. They can connect you with people who matter, guide you on making your project larger, or even connect you with people willing to put money in your idea. Having mentors involved in setting up any challenge is really important because it helps a lot. Maybe you bring them out when it is very important, and you're prepared to your best 5 or 10 teams. One, if they so choose, may ponder why mentors are such of significant consequence, they're an interesting combination of intelligent and informed coaches and industry insiders that might help a team turn a special skill into something extremely functional and important.

Recruiting participants is another critical component. A successful hackathon benefits from a diverse group of participants, bringing together individuals with different skills, backgrounds, and perspectives. Effective promotion through social media, industry networks, and educational institutions can help attract a wide range of participants. It's also beneficial to establish criteria for participation to ensure that attendees are committed and capable of contributing meaningfully to the competition. Givemechallenge also offers paid promotional service for innovation competitions so that we promote your competition to people so that they know about the opportunity.

To keep the hackathon on track, establish a clear framework for idea generation and development.

If it is a public challenge, the initial ideas submitted by people are crucial to the challenge and the new participants will look forward to it like role model ideas for them to easily understand the brief and submit, some people don't even read the brief of the challenge, they blindly go based on what initial ideas are submitted and submit ideas on similar lines, so feedback on initial ideas at least is crucial to put the hackathon on track towards the goal. I have seen many innovation challenges were people come and submit ideas that is no way closer to the challenge brief and the new people who onboard look into these ideas and submit ideas which are more aligned to initial ideas than the brief of the challenge. A chocolate company would be looking for a packaging innovation for their chocolate and the participants might come and submit an idea for a new type of chocolate altogether in this case the ideas doesn't serve the purpose of the challenge.

To run a smooth event, it's a must to lay out crystal-clear rules about what pitches need to cover, such as the issue being solved, the proposed answer to that issue, and how it's going to be put into action. Making sure there's a plan for teams to regularly meet up with mentors and hit certain goals during the event can push them forward. Giving them material they need to brainstorm and build their plans, such as outlines, methods, and programs, will make it easier for everyone to get their thoughts straight and their projects going. It's intelligent and informed to rope in people who know their material to judge the projects; they should look at each project based on different things such as originality, do ability, a type of impact, and how well it's done. Everybody should know how a judging works ahead of time to keep it all above board, which helps make sure nobody thinks it's unfair.

Teams should write down their thinking and choices as they go, seeing how an idea starts and changes into a finalized project can shine a significant quotient of light on the whole notion. The grand finale of a project is when everyone demonstrates what they've come up with and tries to sell their solutions to the judges or the important people watching. Having professionals lead workshops on how to make their presentations snappier can up the chances of people getting their points across much more clearly. The undertaking strived to catch the brightest ideas by sifting through the clutter with a rock-solid, unbiased manner of judging that crucially values how fresh, workable, impactful, and well-crafted each idea is. Judges with a broad range of knowledge bring a balanced view, obtaining each pitch to find those who knocked it out of the park.

You might find it hard to believe but keeping the names behind ideas secret really levels the playing ground when it comes to judging them fairly. If the people looking at the ideas don't know who's who, they focus more on what the proposal's actually about instead of getting caught on who came up with it. This is really cool because it means everyone gets a fair chance, no matter their background or previous achievements – it's all about how good your idea is. What's really wonderful is, when nobody worries about being unfairly judged, a significant amount more people from all sorts of backgrounds are willing to join in. This often leads to a lot of unique and interesting ideas that might not have surfaced otherwise.

Not knowing who's behind what promotes a setting where the most impressive, most useful solutions shine because of how great they are, not because of who submitted them. It's a solid way to make sure the winners truly earned their spot. This anonymous setup might not work for every little contest but it makes a large difference in larger challenges, especially when the goal is to capture the top ideas from a large group of people. And to tell the truth, having several different people making the calls instead of just two or three ensures everything is fairer all around. I've seen many situations where extremely deserving projects (mine included) got overlooked because the people deciding were, we could say, less than impartial. Making sure everyone's ideas get a fair look, regardless of where they came from, protects the contest's integrity and keeps things legitimate.

At its most basic level, essentially what we're saying is if we have a contest like a creative challenge or a coding competition, making the judging crew larger than just a few people can actually improve things a lot. When several people with different skills and views come together to judge, they share many different ideas, which means they're significantly more likely to be fair and not only pick favourites based on their personal likes. Because when you have many judges, you have many people looking at every part of what's being put down. This is extremely key because it cuts down on the chance of anyone's personal take skewing the results too much. This idea banks on the wisdom of the crowd, which is just a special way of saying a significant quotient of brains working together are probably going to make smarter calls than just a couple would.

Adding to that, with more judges on board, we increase the variety of backgrounds. We get individuals from different walks of life, different jobs, and they've got all sorts of wisdom to share, which only makes the decision about who has the best idea much clearer and better. In addition, by pulling in a larger group, we avoid the uncomfortable feeling of having judges and competitors being too friendly or, weird scenario, been in the same campus club last year.

Let's say there's a team in the finals from University X, and someone from the same location is judging. That right there could make things unfair easily if there are teams from University Y and University Z in the mix too but when the judge pool is very large, risks like these drops, because it's less likely any single judge's bias or mates will make things unbalanced. Bumping up the number of judges doesn't only level the playing field, it actually helps make sure the truly amazing ideas move forward quickly and receive the awards they deserve.

If there is a cash prize or an award that is provided to the participant it is important to make sure the participant is aware of a tentative timeline by which the award will be credited to the winner, I know these are small things but these are the basics that could improve the experience of the participants in an innovation competition. The reason I am mentioning this here is because since Givemechallenge aggregates and post the information about various innovation competition, even though we are just a medium providing the information, I have seen many cases where the winners have reached out to us due to delay in prizes and some even asking us if those challenges were a scam or real.

After everything wraps up, don't simply stop there. Keeping the tenor going is key. You could connect people with people who might want to invest in their ideas, get them spots in incubator programs or set up more discussion with mentors. And don't forget to support what everyone accomplished and put those wins in the area for everyone to see. It makes a ripple effect, getting more people to start using new and creative ideas, tracking where ideas start and how they shift and grow tells us a lot about getting marvellous things off the ground. By doing this, we figure out what makes some ideas stick and others flop. It is moreover apparent to you and this paves the way for even more amazing events in the future.

CHAPTER XIV

How Governments Are Using Innovation for Better Governance

Crowdsourcing for ideation

The Indian government have taken various innovative initiatives in India to solve various problems, some of them are mentioned here, I have skipped the obvious and the popular ones and would like to draw your attention to less known innovations.

PM mementos portal: - In India Prime Minister used to receive various expensive and attractive gifts from across organizations and countries, ideally this is a big conflict of interest, so the government was looking for ways to utilize these memorabilia for public good. It is also interesting to note that some gifts which are less expensive, once it is given to the PM the value of the product goes up significantly, that is how PM mementos portal and initiative was started, where all the gifts received by Prime Minister Shri Narendra Modi is auctioned off, where public can bid for it, every time a new bidder bids the price goes up and auction extension timer resets increasing the auction time, this uncertainty in closing auction price and competition helps to raise funds through these auctions. Another big problem that India was facing was pollution of river ganga, people of India were directly responsible for this menace so it was apt to use the funds generated from PM mementos in cleaning up river ganga which is known as Namami Ganga Project. I have mentioned this project here as I have also used this portal twice and collected a few mementos too and I can't stop appreciating this innovation.

Neem coating of urea: - In 2015, the Government of India took a transformational decision to introduce 100 % neem coating on all subsidized agricultural grade urea in the country. All the indigenous and imported urea were neem coated so as to make the urea slow release and difficult to use for non-agricultural purposes. Earlier people used to misuse this benefit by selling the subsidized urea obtained from government to paint and plywood companies instead of agricultural use.

The Soil health card scheme:- Agricultural jobs account for 43.96 percent of India's workforce in 2021, so this scheme made total sense. A Soil Health Card is used to assess the current status of soil health and when used over time, to determine changes in soil health resulting from land management. Using a Soil Health Card, you can see soil health indicators and descriptive terms. It lists soil health indicators that can be assessed without the use of technical or laboratory equipment. Most of them are based on farmers' practical experience and knowledge of local natural resources.

Soil Health Card (SHC) is a Government of India's scheme promoted by the Department of Agriculture & Co-operation under the Ministry of Agriculture and Farmers' Welfare. It is being implemented through the Department of Agriculture of all the State and Union Territory Governments. A lot of farmers in India don't know what to grow to get maximum yield, so the Soil Health Card Scheme is a great idea. Basically, they don't know the quality and the type of their soil. They might know from experience what crops grow and what crops don't. But they don't know what to do to improve the soil so this scheme was very useful.

Mygov.in:- Have you ever wondered how come government come up with very innovative names, slogans and logos for various programs and schemes of the government. This is where MyGov platform comes in, MyGov is an innovative platform to build a partnership between Citizens and Government with the help of technology for growth and development of India. I covered this in detail in my previous chapter.

Here citizens can participate in various crowdsourcing competition and get rewarded, various small challenges are posted here including naming of various schemes, slogan writing competition and logo designing for various government programs. So by crowdsourcing that is leveraging the power of crowd great innovations can be generated even if it is as simple as naming a program or scheme of the government.

ENAM:- To create a unified national market for agricultural commodities, National Agriculture Market (eNAM) is an electronic trading portal that connects all the existing APMC mandis in India. Small Farmers Agribusiness Consortium (SFAC) is the lead agency for implementing eNAM under the aegis of the Ministry of Agriculture and Farmers' Welfare, Government of India.

Streamlining procedures across integrated markets, reducing information asymmetry between buyers and sellers, and promoting real-time price discovery. Through a common online market platform, this project aims to integrate APMCs throughout the country to facilitate pan-India agriculture trade by facilitating better price discovery through transparent auctions based on product quality and timely online payments. On the e-NAM platform, over 1.75 crore farmers and 2.43 lakh traders have registered (as on March 31, 2023)

Farmers used to sell their produce at auction in APC mandis, so they brought it to the market. In this initiative, the government solved the problem of price hoarding, where farmers hoarded commodities and artificially inflated prices. As well as addressing and reverse the fragmentation of markets, NAM also aims to lower intermediation costs, waste and prices.

Atal Innovation Mission (AIM):- Government of India's flagship initiative is the Atal Innovation Mission (AIM), which promotes innovation and entrepreneurship across the country. Using real-time MIS systems and dynamic dashboards, AIM develops new programmes and policies to foster innovation in various sectors of the economy, provides platforms and collaboration opportunities for different stakeholders, and creates an umbrella structure to all the initiatives of AIM. For continuous improvement, AIM's programs are also being reviewed by third parties.

Atal Tinkering Labs - at school level is an AIM program. By using 21st century tools and technologies like Internet of Things, 3D printing, rapid prototyping tools, robotics, miniaturized electronics, do-it-yourself kits and more, ATL is a state-of-the-art space established in a school to foster curiosity and innovation in students in grades 6 to 12. It's about stimulating problem-solving and innovation in children of the ATL and nearby communities. AIM has set up 10,000 Atal Tinkering Labs in schools so far.

Atal Incubation Centres - Building Startups and Entrepreneurs ecosystem of India

Incubation centers, or AICs, are business incubators set up by AIM at universities, institutions, and corporations to encourage innovation and entrepreneurship. With 72 Atal Incubation Centres across India, AIM aims to foster world-class innovation and support entrepreneurs who want to build scalable and sustainable companies. The AICs provide technical facilities, resource-based support, mentorship, funding support, partnerships, networking, coworking spaces, lab facilities, and more to startups. More than 3500 startups are incubated at these AICs, which have created 32000 jobs. More than 1000 startups are led and founded by women. Among the things AICs support are HealthTeach, Fintech, EdTech, Space and Drone Tech, AR/VR, Food Processing, and

Tourism. See the country's innovation & entrepreneurship ecosystem.

By supporting bussing innovation at grass root level like schools to bring out many innovative products & services in the country makes this program innovative.

As mentioned earlier there are numerous govt initiatives like UPI which is highly innovative and revolutionary but I have not included these since it is already popular and well known to the public, here are a few more less known innovation by government, some the schemes are getting adopted by other countries too. One such initiative was Nigeria seeks India's help to emulate Jan Aushadhi Kendra model. Through this book my intention is make such schemes that has potential to be scaled across country and adopted in developed and developing countries outside Bharat too.

PM-WANI:- With PM-WANI, Broadband will be provided via public WiFi hotspots. Public Data Offices (PDOs), Public Data Office Aggregators (PDOAs), App Providers, and Central Registry are the elements. This framework takes forward the goal of the National Digital Communications Policy, 2018 (NDCP) to create a robust digital communications infrastructure by allowing public hotspots to be accessed. A PM-WANI framework aims to provide Broadband through Public Wi-Fi Hotspots. One needs to download an App that shows the available networks. It will consist of elements like the Public Data Office (PDO), Public Data Office Aggregator (PDOA), App Provider and Central Registry. The App will show all the available networks when the user reaches a public Wi-Fi hotspot. Choose a Public Wi-Fi network, pay an amount online or through a voucher, and use the network until the balance runs out.To facilitate ease of doing business and encourage local shops and small establishments to become Wi-Fi providers, it has been approved that the last-mile Public Wi-Fi providers require no license, no registration and will not need to pay any fees to DoT."

In fact, PDOAs, who will aggregate the last-mile providers will also not require any license. These PDOAs will only have to register, for which no fees will be charged. The registration process will be completed within 7 working days of the receipt of applications.

Gem:- GeM is a one-stop Government eMarket Place hosted by DGS&D where common goods and services can be procured. GeM is dynamic, self-sustaining, and user-friendly portal for Government officials to make procurements. Government procurement is a big part of what they do, and reforming it is one of the top priorities right now. Government e-Marketplace (GeM) is a bold step taken by the Government with the aim of transforming how the Government Ministry and Department procures goods and services, as well as Public Sector Undertakings and other apex autonomous bodies. The major problem is corruption, because there was always corruption when buying various products, where tax payers money was used to buy stuff at high prices, but with this portal, vendors have to offer a competitive price and everything's transparent and visible to the public, so it's cheaper to buy these things.

GeM (Government e-Marketplace) offers a comprehensive solution for government procurement buyers and sellers. With GeM, buyers get a rich listing of products and services across various categories, making it easy to search, compare, select, and buy online. Also, buyers get quality assurance and accountability thanks to continuous vendor rating systems. For sellers, GeM acts as a one-stop shop for marketing with minimal effort because it's direct access to all government departments. You can show off your stuff, bid on it, and suggest new stuff. In addition, they get a seller-friendly dashboard that lets them manage supplies, payments, and sales performance, along with dynamic pricing. The GeM's consistent and uniform purchase procedures foster efficiency, transparency, and fairness, facilitating seamless transactions and fostering a vibrant government procurement market.

A Journey's End, A New Beginning

URGENT PLEA!

Thank You For Reading My Book!

I really appreciate all of your feedback and

I love hearing what you have to say

I need your input to make the next version of this book and my future books better. Please take two minutes now to leave a helpful review on Amazon letting me know what you thought of the book, Optionally you can also leave a private review here.

• • •

Givemechallenge.com/BreakingIdeas
Thanks so much!
- Aadhithya
Email:- givemechallenge@yahoo.com
Website:- Givemechallenge.com